CULTURE, IDENTITY AND BROADCASTING IN IRELAND

Local Issues, Global Perspectives

This publication has received support from
Cultural Traditions Group of the
Community Relations Council.

Culture, Identity and Broadcasting in Ireland

Local Issues, Global Perspectives

**Proceedings of the Cultural Traditions Group/
Media Studies UUC
Symposium, 21 February, 1991**

Edited, with an Introduction
by
Martin McLoone

Institute of Irish Studies
The Queen's University of Belfast

The cover illustration is entitled 'Stalemate' and is reproduced by kind permission of the artist, Gerry Gleason.

First published 1991
by the Institute of Irish Studies
The Queen's University of Belfast
University Road, Belfast

ISBN 0 85389 409 4

Printed by W. & G. Baird Ltd, Antrim

CONTENTS

PREFACE

Part II of this volume presents the proceedings of the symposium 'Culture, Identity and Broadcasting in Ireland – Local Issues, Global Perspectives' which was hosted by the Media Studies section of the University of Ulster at Coleraine on February 21st, 1991 and which was sponsored by the Cultural Traditions Group, a sub-committee of the Community Relations Council.

I want to thank all those who attended the symposium and who contributed to the discussions. In particular I want to express my gratitude to Professor Philip Schlesinger for agreeing to give the keynote address and to the rest of the speakers for agreeing to give discussion papers.

My thanks also to the staff at the University of Ulster, especially my colleagues in Media Studies, for ensuring that the symposium proceeded smoothly, efficiently and enjoyably.

Both the symposium and the publication were funded by the Cultural Traditions Group and I thank them for their generosity. The whole venture was facilitated by Maurna Crozier whose advice was invaluable.

A special word of thanks to James Hawthorne, Chairman of the Community Relations Council, not only for supporting the project from the beginning but also for giving generously of his time in chairing one session and contributing so pertinently and with considerable wit and candour, to the other sessions.

In Part I, I have written an introductory essay in which I try to summarise the historical background to the issues discussed in the symposium and offer my own analysis of the European context in which they operate. The broadcasting environment is changing so quickly and the political landscape of Europe evolving so rapidly that the analysis and suggestions offered here are necessarily tentative. My hope is that they will, at least, stimulate further discussion on a range of issues which I believe will continue to dominate cultural politics in Ireland, Britain and the rest of Europe for many years to come.

The Introduction draws on a larger research project in which I am engaged. The historical research was funded by the British Academy and the continuing project is supported by the Faculty of Humanities at the University of Ulster.

The symposium proceedings were transcribed from tape recordings, and the whole manuscript nursed through to publication stage, by Janetta Chambers.

Finally my thanks to Cindy, Katie and Maeve for their encouragement and support, knowing and unwitting, and my deep gratitude to them for giving me a year out.

PART I

INTRODUCTION

Inventions and Re-imaginings : Some thoughts on Identity and Broadcasting in Ireland

by

Martin McLoone

Inventions and Re-imaginings : Some thoughts on Identity and Broadcasting in Ireland

Martin McLoone

1. A Unionist in Dail Eireann

It is my very deep and profound conviction . . . that we cannot set up a Chinese wall around the country, or establish an exclusive civilization. If we wish to do that, let there be no wireless broadcasting . . . In the past – the distant past – we influenced Europe profoundly and I hope it will be our lot to so again. We shall not do it by pursuing a policy of isolation and by shutting out the education that comes from European civilization.[1]

These words were spoken in Dail Eireann on February 15th 1924 by Major Bryan Cooper, Independent T.D. for Co. Dublin. The occasion was a debate on the Second Interim Report of the Special Committee established by the Dail to investigate the structures and financing of a broadcasting service for the Free State. What is significant about this debate is that, while ostensibly it was concerned with the mechanisms for establishing a broadcasting service, in reality it broadened out to address wider issues of broadcast policy and its relationship to cultural identity.

In particular, the debate was concerned with the potential of broadcasting to mediate and promote notions of national consciousness as well as its power to disseminate cultural expression and values from outside.

It was, then, an early example of a debate which is at the centre of contemporary cultural politics. Indeed, it may even rank as an historical landmark every bit as significant as that other broadcasting 'first' often attributed to Ireland – the first ever broadcast itself, beamed out to the airwaves in morse from the GPO in 1916.[2] For at the centre of the debate lie the aspirations of an emerging post-colonial nation and its apprehensions about a form of cultural imperialism associated with the power of broadcasting, only half-glimpsed at the time, but nonetheless clearly enunciated.

It was, then, an early and historically specific expression of issues which, in their contemporary forms, are contested in advanced industrial societies as well as in the pauperised third world; within nation-states, between nation-states and transnationally across the globe. Indeed this very global prominence had given a renewed energy to just such specifically local issues and the experience of the local, in its historical as well as in its contemporary dimensions, has now begun to feed back into global perspectives.

The debate about identity in Ireland, then, whilst sometimes it may have seemed like a pointless exercise in xenophobic navel-gazing, now appears to be at the cutting-edge of contemporary discourse. In this regard, Bryan Cooper's long-forgotten words in a dimly recalled debate, strike me as being both deeply poignant and uncannily prescient.

Cooper had been a Unionist M.P. for Co. Dublin at Westminster before the Treaty and in his words one can sense today perhaps, a man resigned to his own historical redundancy. And yet his contribution to the broadcasting debate, sometimes flippant or acerbic, at other times idealistic and aspirational, now seem peculiarly relevant.

Cooper's intervention had been prompted by comments made earlier in the debate by the Postmaster General, J.J. Walsh. Walsh had warned that in failing to implement his own scheme for establishing broadcasting (an Irish commercial concern under the control of native private enterprise) the Dail ran the risk of turning the airwaves over to 'British music hall dope and British propaganda.'[3] By way of response, Cooper acerbically declared, 'I am afraid that if we are to have wireless broadcasting established on an exclusively Irish – Ireland basis, the result will be *Danny Boy* four times a week, with variations by way of camouflage.'[4]

Like his Ulster Unionist contemporaries, Cooper was motivated by a fear of the exclusivist definitions of Irish cultural identity which were shaping society around him. Indeed, he had the foresight to see that such exclusivity was ultimately self-destructive and the poignancy of his words for a contemporary observer stems from the fact that 'the Chinese Wall' which he warned about was indeed constructed around the new state and Ireland entered a forty year period of economic and cultural isolation.

The new medium of radio broadcasting was mobilised (albeit in a particularly penny-pinching manner) behind the cultural project of nation-building. In a famously wry judgement, Maurice Gorham said of Irish radio in the decades following its inauguration –

> "It was expected not merely to reflect every aspect of national activity, but to create activities which did not exist. It was expected to revive the speaking of Irish; to keep people on the farms; to sell goods and services of all kinds from sausages to sweep tickets; to provide a living and a career for writers and musicians; to re-unite the Irish people at home with those overseas; to end partition."[5]

Unlike his Ulster Unionist contemporaries and (more to the point) their descendants today, Cooper's solution to the exclusivist thrust of Irish nationalism was not to run for cover within the embrace of an equally essentialist British/Unionist identity. Rather his response was to invoke a form of European common consciousness. This response reflected, of course, his own background and education – his social class – driving him to embrace a European sense of identity and to urge a form of broadcasting which would reflect the high art achievements of European civilization (*Hamlet*, for example, but if this reeked too much of 'British music-hall dope', he also suggested *Parsifal* and Glazounov).[6] Cooper's attempts to enlarge the local/particular onto a European stage is a strategy which would command considerable support in contemporary Ireland, north and south, as I discuss in more detail below.

Indeed what is remarkable about the whole debate is that it touches on a number of key elements which have become crucial to contemporary concerns about culture and national consciousness. Cooper, for example, alludes to the fundamental relationship between the growth and promotion of collective identities and the process of communication, speculating with remarkable prescience about the particular relationship between identity and the new broadcasting medium. He manages to allude to the core/periphery relationship of indigenous culture within this process and to tease out a tripartite relationship involving Irish, British and European formulations of collective consciousness, which has a particularly contemporary resonance. Finally he raises a deeper, more philosophical question about the nature of identity itself, setting up a contrast between definitions of identity which are posed in essentialist terms against those promulgated through larger, more pluralist formulations.

These three elements, of course, interconnect in deeply complex ways, but they tend to manifest themselves in everyday life in ways which can be both banal and tragic. Contemporary Ireland is only too familiar with this banality and this tragedy and for broadcasting, they raise fundamental questions.

Should RTE, for example, continue to give prominence in its radio and television schedules to *The Angelus,* a Catholic devotional prayer? How should the BBC in Northern Ireland regard the Twelfth of July parades? How does broadcasting in Ireland today contribute, however unwittingly, to a climate that sustains horrific sectarian killings? How can it contribute to a climate of reconciliation?

Now it would be foolish to regard broadcasting as the prime mover in the banalities and the tragedies of contemporary Ireland – in the end one must look for explanations and for solutions in historical, economic and social contexts. But at the basis of intercommunal strife in Ireland, there lies a conflict over identity and for better or worse, communications play a central role in the formation of identity. Broadcasting, in particular, is crucial in mediating and sustaining a sense of collective consciousness.

Bryan Cooper's voice in 1924 was that of a disappearing southern Irish unionism. His words provide an eloquent epitaph by throwing down a challenge to contemporary Ireland. His comments on the dangers inherent in 'an exclusive civilization' were well made (a little too late, one hastens to add, for the class and culture which spawned him – nothing became the Anglo-Irish ascendancy more than the manner of its leaving the stage of history). But perhaps his fate, and his aspirations, allow us to approach the whole question of identity with rather more openness, and with a greater sense of complexity, than either nationalism or unionism did in his day, or the more recidivist elements of both continue to do today.

2. 'Shrunken Imaginings of Recent History'

There is an ironic, contradictory thrust about Europe in the 1990's which provides an interesting perspective on Ireland's 'ancient quarrels'. On one hand, the twelve member states of the European Community move inexorably towards closer economic and political union while middle and east European states, formerly under Soviet hegemony, pull asunder and demand even greater national autonomy. Yugoslavia, for example, is the latest state to implode with conflicting and violent ethnic tensions.

What both developments have done is to re-insert into political and cultural discourse the whole question of national and ethnic identity. The return of nationalism and the related questions about statehood, national rights and ethnic minority rights form once again the central political question in Europe. It is in this sense, then, that the debates in contemporary Ireland no longer seem to be the obsolete lingerings of an irrelevant conflict – 'the integrity of their quarrel'[7] is once again being played out on a global stage.

I think what this allows us to do is to place the questions about identity in Ireland into a wider context – to draw lessons from the global perspective and to view the conflicts of identity here not in their uniqueness, but in their universality.

It is, of course, a highly complex set of issues and there is a considerable body of literature available which looks at it from a variety of perspectives – historical, economic, political, cultural, sociological, anthropological and psychological.[8] It is impossible to consider this range of academic theory here, but I want to acknowledge its existence to make one fundamental observation about Ireland. For far too long, conceptions about identity in Ireland have been conducted on a purely one-dimensional plane, operating at a disablingly simplistic level around the competing formulations of Irishness and Britishness, both of which are posed in essentialist terms.

What this has meant in political terms (and one cannot divorce the question of identity from politics) is that in Ireland after 1921, two states emerged in which the essentialist formulations of Irishness and Britishness dictated social and economic policy, forging a politic which was insular, stifling, oppressive and intoler-ant of difference. (Indeed, the experience raises the question of the relationship between *cultural nationalism* and *political national-ism* which, despite the huge literature available, seems to me to be too little discussed and largely under-theorised.) This had pro-found implications for the development and character of broad-casting in Ireland as I discuss below.

These essentialist formulations are now under severe pressure in both states, rent asunder internally by the contradictions which they could no longer contain and challenged fundamentally by the external pressures of global trends (the internationalisation of capital, the transnational nature of communications and, of course, the implications for Ireland and the U.K. of EC membership). This allows us, then, to reconsider the ways in which we might think about identity and perhaps delineate the potential which now exists for working our way out of an historical impasse.

In an influential study of nationalism, Benedict Anderson offered the following formulation:

> The nation is an imagined political community – and imagined as both inherently limited and sovereign.[9]

I want to appropriate here, Anderson's formulation because it seems to me to offer a suggestive framework for understanding the basis of collective consciousness and the means for clarifying how we might in Ireland, begin to address our conflict over identity.

At its most simple, Anderson's formulation allows us to see clearly the fact that identities are forged by human endeavour, rather than the result of divine ordinance. Identity is *artefact* and not *nature.* This would negate the dominant thrust of national movements, as nationalists perceive it – the pursuit of essence, as I have referred to it elsewhere.[10] It does not, however negate the *political* need for such a strategy which is often articulated by subaltern cultures seeking to overthrow the political control of more powerful cultures. It does however, suggest that this pursuit flies in the face of material reality and in the contradiction between the essentialist endeavour and this reality, there lie many dangers, not least the potential for self-delusion and for intercommunal conflict. For this sense of an imagined community also suggests a range of other characteristics, in relation to the nature of identity:

- It is a process and therefore is dynamic rather than static
- The imagining of identity involves a process of inclusion and exclusion (to arrive at what Anderson calls 'inherently limited').
- Because it is dynamic, what is included today can be excluded tomorrow and vice versa.
- If identities are imagined in Anderson's sense of the word, then they can be imagined differently; crucially for my purposes they can be *re-imagined* in the light of changed economic and social contexts.
- Identities are forged in a dialectic between 'us' and 'them' – between a negotiation of internal factors and external influences, especially in relation to the centre/periphery relationship.[11]
- Identities are, therefore, intensely problematic, contradictory and constantly in flux.

It seems to me, then, that nationalist conceptions of identity, the pursuit of essence, is necessarily contingent on a less complex formulation. For nationalisms engaged in political struggle, the crucial project is a *hegemonic* one, attempting to imagine a line of connection against the grain of others (class, gender, religion, geography and so on). It is a project, therefore, which must suppress at least as much as it liberates, and create an image of 'the other' to reinforce the legitimacy of 'us'. 'These shrunken imaginings of recent history', as Anderson dubs them, create in the process, a language of abuse, as well as language of love, and terms like 'traitor', 'collaborator', and 'alien' have assumed deep and sinister meanings. In the specific contexts of all nationalisms, there are dozens of such loaded pejoratives, fixed within one context by their equivalents in the 'other'.

In a larger sense, then, it might be suggestive at least, to consider the formation of identity, whether national, ethnic, religious or sub-group, as essentially a *cultural* process (ie the result of human endeavour). Thus *all* identities are *cultural identities*. This is not to deny the ideological, political or economic underpinnings of collective imaginings – in their status as artefact and not nature, the interplay of such materialist forces is assumed. Rather it is to acknowledge that identities are forms of communication expressed through sets of social practices and the acceptance of agreed language, symbols and rituals.

This brings us to a second useful formulation which operates in the same vein as Anderson's *imagined communities*. In considering how certain rituals, symbols and social practices evolve, Eric Hobsbawm describes a process which he dubs 'the invention of tradition'.

'Invented tradition' is taken to mean a set of practices normally governed by overtly or tacitly accepted rules and of a ritual or symbolic nature, which seek to inculcate certain values and norms of behaviour by repetition, which automatically implies continuity with the past. In fact, where possible, they normally attempt to establish continuity with a suitable past . . . in so far as there is such reference to a historic past, the peculiarity of 'invented traditions' is that the continuity with it is largely factitious.[12]

In surveying the mass-production of such 'traditions' in Europe, Hobsbawm puts special emphasis on the years 1870–1914, a period exactly coterminous with the consolidation in Ireland of the essentialist formulations of Irish nationalism and Ulster unionism. Most of the key symbolic rituals of both can be traced back only as far as this crucial historical moment. But Hobsbawm's formulation is suggestive for two further reasons.

Firstly, the invention of tradition perfectly sums up the relationship that identity-formation has with history. History is like a 'rag-and-bone-shop' which can be ransacked at certain key political moments for usable garb which is then dusted-off, re-fitted and worn to meet particular needs. If the desired result is a form of collective memory, it can only work by insisting on a form of collective amnesia as well. The end result is 'myth', in the sense which Barthes understood it – reality purged of history and politics and rendered as some kind of commonsense.[13]

Secondly, I feel that the invention of tradition very precisely describes the particular role that broadcasting has played in the formation and maintenance of collective consciousness in the period *after* that which Hobsbawm emphasises. The thrust of broadcasting's role, in both Britain and Ireland, has been towards a denial of the complexities and dynamics of cultural identity. It has attempted, through its own ransacking of the rag-and-bone-shop of history, to fix and to freeze a certain notion of identity. It has selected and discarded, remembered and forgotten, invented and imagined in ways which have coincided with, if not always been directed by, the needs of the nation-states. In the process it has evolved as a central cultural agency for the promotion of collective consciousness.

With these more complex notions of identity in mind, I want therefore, to return to the question of broadcasting and in particular to consider the history and present condition of public service broadcasting in Britain and in Ireland.

3. Public Service Broadcasting and the 'Big We'

. . . I would like to wish continued success and prosperity to broadcasting in the Irish Free State. While the primary mission of broadcasting is to serve the people, it has also – and perhaps in no less a degree – to serve the peoples, and the programme arrangements now in force between the Irish organisation and our own are not only an index of our happy relations, but a beginning of the still wider interchange which is foreshadowed in the BBC motto: 'Nation shall speak peace unto Nation'. John Reith, Director General of the BBC, 1927 [14]

Each stage in the development of communications – whether transport, informational or symbolic – has everywhere given a boost to the process of defining national or ethnic consciousness. Benedict Anderson, for example, has delineated the way in which the invention of printing and the spread of literacy was central to the spread of Protestantism in early modern Europe. A by-product of this was the increased interest in and emphasis on vernacular languages and vernacular cultures which was to prove crucial in delineating the boundaries of collective consciousness.[15] In the nineteenth century, the rise of mass circulation newspapers and mass-produced pamphlets was equally important for the spread of nationalism in South America and across Europe.[16]

In the twentieth century though, broadcasting has been the primary site for the mediation, promotion and maintenance of collective identity. In this regard, the experience of public service broadcasting throughout Europe is crucial. The BBC was, to some extent, the role model here and, with slight inflections to meet local needs, the model was adopted throughout Europe. David Cardiff and Paddy Scannell have shown how the BBC in its formative years, set out, in John Reith's words 'to make the nation as one man'. The important dimension of this process was broadcasting's ability to mediate to all corners of the state, the symbolic rituals of the centre (whether the monarch's Christmas message, days of solemn remembrance or sporting occasions like the F.A. Cup Final).[17] These are all key examples in Hobsbawm's list of British 'invented traditions'.

If these annual rituals of collective consciousness have formed a central thread of British public service broadcasting, then the mode of address which is characteristic of them has penetrated all other areas of the schedules, not least news and current affairs.[18] The smiling, all-inclusive embrace of this broadcasting address (which I call 'the big We') operates, of course, to forge a sense of collective identity across the potentially divisive factors of class, gender, regional or ethnic background and a host of other particularities. In this sense then, public service broadcasting has always operated a form of masking, forging links by denying (or at least playing down) difference. It is a hegemonic project, in line with the essentialist formulations of national consciousness which I have outlined above.

However it must also be noted that, whatever the deeper complexities of identity which were thus hidden, British public service broadcasting was successful in its hegemonic thrust only in so far as it reflected a sense of common consciousness – Britishness – which commanded, at least superficially, some degree of popular consensus. British public service broadcasting therefore has always been 'consensus' broadcasting.[19]

It has, as well, been a cultural manifestation of the liberal or social democratic thrust of the British state itself, and became a key site for mediating and promoting its underlying ideology. Consensus broadcasting has also, therefore, been an intensely contradictory phenomenon. On one hand, in its pursuit of hegemony, it has operated as a rather blunt instrument, legitimising (and marginalising) forms of public discourse by patrolling the boundaries of accepted social, political and cultural behaviour. And yet since its formative days under Reith's guidance, it has always striven to maintain its autonomy from government interference and from the influences of the market place. Thus in its commitment to impartiality and its obligation to represent all sections of society it has also provided a space for the kinds of dissident or minority opinion which in its hegemonic role, it sought to disavow.

It seems to me, therefore, important to draw a clear distinction between the *ethos* or *principle* of public service broadcasting and the institutions, and the performance of those institutions, charged with its operation (the BBC initially, but also the Independent network which later emerged). It is this ethos which has been British social democracy's contribution to broadcasting philosophy – the principle indeed which has allowed at least the *potential* for a more democratic and more accountable broadcasting system to be envisaged. This ethos also allows the potential for more radical, more complex formulations of cultural identity to emerge.

In this regard, and despite its commercial funding, the arrival of Channel Four in 1982, now appears as the high point of British public service broadcasting – the apotheosis of a system whose public service ethos is guaranteed on the one hand by regulated market forces and on the other by a privileged place above them.

Of course the whole structure and basic philosophy of public service broadcasting has come under great strain in recent years.

Throughout the 1980s a British government hostile to all kinds of public service and committed to a market-led economy coincided with a crisis in revenue and a proliferation in commercial competition from new broadcast technologies. The future of the institutions and their underlying ethos is now a matter of some concern, which is touched on by many of the contributors below.

However the British model of public service broadcasting has faced difficulties in Ireland, north and south, for a lot longer than this. Despite Reith's optimistic message about British and Irish broadcasting in 1927, the dice was already loaded against the prospect of 'nation speaking peace unto nation'.

In Northern Ireland, of course, broadcasting is directly part of the British system, but the peculiar nature of society in the north has thrown this very system into crisis. For example, as David Butler has argued, there are few 'national' occasions in the British broadcast calendar which remain uncontested in the north (the F.A. Cup Final is perhaps one of the few). In a society which patently lacks the kind of consensus which underpins, and is promoted by, this cyclical display of national unity, local broadcasting, especially BBC NI, has had to tread a different path from the network models.[20]

The dissensual nature of Northern Ireland society is manifested in the very language of identification itself. As David Butler graphically explains below, 'All the signifiers are spoken for'. This means that recurring problems for broadcasting – how to cover the Twelfth of July parades (as 'national' celebration, folk festival or deeply divisive political/sectarian event?) or how to refer to the north's second largest city (Derry or Londonderry?) – are banal at one level but in their deeply symbolic significance, indicative of the tragedy of the situation as well.

Faced with such banality and such tragedy British public service broadcasting in Northern Ireland has veered from the consensus model, at one time promulgating both government opinion and dominant Unionist culture and at another time presenting itself as a kind of 'honest broker' between two warring factions. In the process it has bowed constantly to forms of direct and indirect censorship which has threatened its very existence as *public service broadcasting*.[21]

In its formative years, the BBC was an important role-model for Irish broadcasting as well. Indeed, the BBC provided the Dublin station with valuable technical help and advice before and after its inauguration on January 1st 1926. But there was a crucial difference, which was to mould the nature of Irish radio for the next thirty years and which continues to pose problems for broadcasting today.

Irish broadcasting was established as a state service, under direct control of the post office, a full year before John Reith was to persuade the British Government to reconstitute the BBC as an autonomous state service.[22] The cultural arguments mobilised in the Dail against private enterprise involvement had won out (against the wishes of the Post Office itself) and Irish broadcasting became one of the first wholly state-controlled services outside the Communist countries. It was, then, in strict terms, public service broadcasting *before* the BBC was.

However, the lack of autonomy which characterised Irish broadcasting under Post Office control laid it open to more direct governmental pressure than the BBC arrangement did (at least the BBC outside of Northern Ireland). Ireland for example has always lacked an uncontested symbolic figure-head, like the British monarch (and extended family) around whom symbolic common identity could be mobilised. In the 1930's and 1940's Eamon de Valera assumed this role for Ireland, especially in terms of broadcast addresses to overseas. Between 1932 and 1946, he made a total of twenty-two such radio broadcasts, mostly to the USA, settling into a pattern of Christmas Day and St. Patrick's Day each year.[23] These broadcasts were bitterly condemned by opposition deputies as blatant party political events and throughout these years there were constant complaints about undue government interference in the affairs of broadcasting.

De Valera's penchant for assuming 'L'état, c'est moi' indicates one crucial difference between broadcasting in Ireland and the British model. Successive Irish governments, but especially Fianna Fail administrations, right down to the present Fianna Fail-led coalition, have always viewed broadcasting's relationship to the state in ways which we might recognise as more Gaullist than strictly Reithian.

Nonetheless, I think it would be fair to say that the Reithian notion of 'making the nation as one man' is the ethos which underlies Irish public service broadcasting as well and from its earliest days it set about the task of uniting its audience around common points of identification. Indeed, as Luke Gibbons has pointed put, the history of Irish broadcasting confirms the truth of

Gorham's wry comments about inventing traditions. The ceili band was a new 'tradition' invented to meet the particular needs of radio broadcasting and radio resuscitated an ailing GAA by providing live coverage of important Gaelic football and hurling events.[24]

In its history, then, one can detect both the fundamental differences and the crucial similarities in the broadcasting systems of both countries. But if anything unites the broadcasting experiences of the north and the south of Ireland today it is the often overlooked fact that *neither* society offers the kind of commonsense national consensus ('unity within diversity' as Cardiff and Scannell would call it) which is at the heart of the British model.

Southern Ireland today is also a deeply fissured society, where competing notions of national identity and cultural tradition vie with one another to dictate political and social policy. There are few uncontested national events and the recent struggle over the 'ownership' and significance of the Easter Rising is only one, albeit telling, manifestation of this. RTE, therefore, operates a public service broadcast system in a society which is deeply divided over definitions of its own identity – a society trying to come to terms with the cultural heritage of Irish-Ireland Catholic nationalism at the same time as it embraces the promise of, and the harsh realities of, a secular, materialist European identity.[25]

The schizophrenia that this induces is illustrated by the perversity of politico/religious discourse in the 1980's. In 1983 and 1986, in two constitutional referenda on abortion and divorce, the country endorsed the moral teachings of the Catholic Church, delivering a significant blow to secular liberal modernisation. And yet, by 1990, the country had elected as president, Mary Robinson, whose whole working life as a feminist/socialist lawyer, has been dedicated to the secularisation of Irish society.

It would be quite wrong, however to characterise RTE's role in this identity crisis as that of honest broker or neutral mediator. Broadcasting in Ireland operates under a public service ethos which I have linked already to a liberal/social democratic ideology. Since the 1960's RTE has been a part of the modernising process in Ireland and has been its primary source of mediation. When Catholic nationalist Ireland complains (as it does continually) that RTE is run by 'the liberal trendies of Dublin 4', I can agree up to a point (and at the same time, have little sympathy for the complaints).

The issue here, of course, is not the influence of mythical Dublin 4 trendies – rather it is the nature of the broadcasting beast itself when it confronts an identity forged is essentialist terms. As Cooper so perceptively noted in 1924, if the cultural project is the maintenance of some exclusivist civilization, better not to have broadcasting at all. For in the end, public service broadcasting, and in the post-war period in particular, public service television, is an outgrowth of a *symptomatic technology*, to use Raymond Williams' phrase[26] – a technology which is developed by a particular form of society and designed to meet the needs of that society.

The requirement to be impartial is crucial here. In its strict adherence to this requirement, broadcasting must always assume that there are at least two sides to any given argument. But an essentialist definition of identity, constructed in exclusivist terms, is above all else, a deeply *authoritarian* concept. The experience of both states in Ireland up to the 1960s is indicative of this authoritarianism.

In the north, nationalist culture was suppressed and Catholics systematically discriminated against in employment and housing and, through gerry-mandering were denied full democratic participation in local government. In the south, the implementation of a particular vision of Catholic Ireland resulted in a society which was deeply conservative in matters relating to private and social morality and constructed around a narrow, rural concept of identity at odds with harsh economic realities. It alienated the urban and forced the disaffected and the dissident into emigration. In both instances, an exclusivist concept of identity dictated social and economic policy and tainted the very structures of civil society with a particular religious ethos.

Broadcasting in these circumstances, developed within an unbending orthodoxy and initially reflected the ethos of this orthodoxy. Thus in the North, the BBC, despite its Reithian principles, reflected only dominant Unionist culture and was effectively the mouthpiece of the Unionist Government.[27] In the South, Radio Eireann was smothered under civil service control and expected to promote unquestioningly the dominant ethos of Catholic Ireland.[28] (This is not to say that there were no frictions or tension between broadcasters and their political/religious masters – there were, and especially in the case of Radio Eireann, these were to provide a process for defining the public service element of broadcasting policy.)

The sea change for both broadcasting services occurred in the late fifties. In the North, commercial broadcasting arrived with the inauguration of Ulster Television in October 1959. Based on commercial criteria, it was imperative that UTV, despite the Unionist conviction of its founding fathers, should acknowledge and attempt to appeal to the one third of the population that was nationalist. As with the BBC nationally, the arrival of commercial broadcasting in Northern Ireland was to stimulate the Corporation into a more populist and more adventurous direction.[29]

In the South, Sean Lemass, who succeeded de Valera in 1959, abandoned the isolationist policies of the previous decades and invited in foreign investment to stimulate a stagnant economy. The result was a steady dismantling of 'the Chinese Wall'. The unhinging of broadcasting from civil service control and the arrival of television in 1961 provided an important communications framework in support of the modernisation process. Broadcasting also became the key agency for mediating the reappraisal of the nationalist project which inevitably followed.

Thus in both states, broadcasting was able to develop more fully its public service ethos, directly and indirectly, tapping more completely into the Reithian ideals which underpin it.

Today, then, both the northern unionist and southern nationalist orthodoxies have collapsed, and in their place there is debate. The residual elements of these exclusivist identities linger on, certainly, and play an important part in the ferment. But public service broadcasting, *by its very nature*, has already taken sides in the disputes, north and south. It is effectively the voice of *secular liberal humanism*, antithetical to the authoritarian impulses of either nationalism or unionism. As such, it leads from the front, promoting and supporting a sense of identity which commands no ready consensus in either society. Were it to do otherwise it would cease to be public service broadcasting as this has historically evolved.

This 'vanguardist' role, as David Butler calls it below, should not be confused with a radical perspective on society. The secular liberal humanism of public service broadcasting is nothing more, nor nothing less, than precisely that. In Ireland north and south its advanced role is relative, when viewed in global terms. It is the absence of consensus, the relatively underdeveloped tradition of liberal or social democratic discourse, which gives broadcasting in Ireland its vanguardist nature. And this is a situation which is as fraught with problems as it is rich in potential.

Let me try to illustrate what I see as the problems by considering briefly the BBC Northern Ireland early evening news programme *Inside Ulster*. For many years *Inside Ulster* operated as a news bulletin/magazine programme/community bulletin board, until recent changes hardened up its news content and moved a lot of the community/magazine elements to specific slots elsewhere on the schedules. Nevertheless, many of the problems discussed here remain. The contrasts I want to outline have merely been shifted across schedules rather than contained within the programme.

The problems stem from the fact that no other region within the BBC's structure has had to deal on a regular basis with such a catalogue of tragedy. Typically, *Inside Ulster's* twenty minute broadcast has been divided between 'hard' news items and 'soft' news stories (the bad news followed by the good). On any given evening, the hard news lead stories have had to report the tragedies of daily life in Northern Ireland – shootings or bombings; killings or maimings; court reports on terrorist trials or convictions for murder; reports on army swoops and arrests; arsenals and bomb factories unearthed. Equally likely has been a litany of condemnations from legitimised authorities (ministers, party leaders, church leaders etc.), seemingly endless as the programme has striven to maintain balance and impartiality. Indeed, in its interviews, and statements broadcast, the programme still continues to be almost arithmetically precise in its search for balance.

The good news is likely to include positive industrial developments (new jobs) or information relating to cultural events or groups with strong cross-community elements (including charity fund-raising events, still a staple item). The contrast, then, could hardly have been greater, the schizophrenia indeed hardly more complete. Now this does reflect a reality, the deeply disturbing truth about Northern Ireland's dissensual society. The problem, I believe, lies in the way the programme has attempted to deal with the contrast, to bridge the gap, to negotiate the contradiction.

For in its vanguardist role, I believe the programme has built each evening *towards* its good news stories – by accentuating the positive and seeking out the consensual, it has attempted not just to balance the negative but to *overwhelm* and render less threatening, the tragedy of the negative.

In other words, I would argue that the programme has attempted to reinforce and build on a marginal centre ground which is humanist and humane, comforting and uplifting, respectful of difference and willing to work in harmony for the greater good. This, I would argue, is the 'big We' of BBC Northern Ireland today.

Now this aim is altogether understandable and laudable, and I would not suggest for a moment that news should go unreported or that inter-community activity is unworthy of public attention. But this operation of consensus broadcasting throws up some anomalies, to say the least. Chief amongst these is the fact that small, relatively unrepresentative, opinion continues to be given disproportionate access to the airwaves. For example, notwith-standing its strength in the south, the Workers' Party in the north is a tiny political grouping but it would find it difficult to argue that its case has not been amply made in programmes like *Inside Ulster*. Likewise the larger, but still marginal Alliance Party.

But the fact that these two determinedly anti-sectarian parties continue to enjoy low (or minuscule) levels of public support suggests that the reinforcing and building role, the vanguardist thrust, of consensus broadcasting has been less than successful. Why? I think there are a number of reasons.

Firstly, it must be said that the liberal humanism of consensus broadcasting has been severely compromised by the restrictions imposed by Government in regard to whose voices it is allowed to give access to in the first place. But I think, anyway, that the whole project is limiting because in the end it is wishful, if not downright utopian. The good news items, 'the big We', represents an act of faith in the sense of humanity which is assumed to lie deep in the hearts of otherwise distrusting and mutually exclusive communi-ties. When this is the dominant mode of address (dominant but not exclusive) across the range of broadcasting's local output, it seriously undervalues the potential which exists for a more chal-lenging approach.

The problem, here, is two-fold. On one hand, the carefully balanced accessed voices give rise to what David Butler has called 'balanced sectarianism'.[30] The hope is that 'good' will overwhelm 'the bad', but all too often the task is beyond it. What we get is a continuation of the 'megaphone politics' of a society which lacks a political forum of any significance. This is exacerbated by the second problem. The Northern Ireland audience is made up in the main of individuals who have learnt how to negotiate the contrast from within their own fixed attitudes. They can be hu-manist and charitable and open in certain situations (like charity promotions) but remain immovable in their political/religious affiliations. They can see 'us and them' more clearly than they can see 'We'.

When the balanced accessed voices and the fixed positions of the audience are both left to stand, the result tends to reinforce the status quo. A belief in the essential goodness of people, or an emphasis on their common humanity, is not enough to move them from fixed ideological perspectives. In other words, this consensus approach leaves the striking contrasts – the macabre contradictions – of Northern Irish society largely unexplored.

Now I do not want to appear overly critical of what is, after all, a twenty-minute news programme. *Inside Ulster* is what it is and on its own terms, it has been working well enough for many years now. I have used it as an exemplar of the public service broadcasting approach, the consensus approach, which throws up these problems when applied to the patently aberrant conditions of Northern Ireland. The 'big We' of this approach is internally contradicted and externally it falls on fallow ground.

Now, as I have already suggested, this is not the exclusive mode of address which emanates from the BBC in Northern Ireland. Mickey McGowan below details a different approach which is utilised by BBC Radio Foyle; David Butler below discusses the 'noble failure' of *The Show* in trying something different and BBC Radio Ulster's *Talkback* has been much discussed.[31] (The fact that all of these, and some recent innovative drama, have been at the centre of considerable controversy, indicates one problem which arises when the audience *is* challenged.)

Finally, many of the criticisms which I make here in relation to the BBC's dominant mode of address could be applied equally to Ulster Television. Consider, for example, this act of faith from UTV's former Managing Director and founding member, Brum Henderson.

> During the height of the troubles we decided fervently to arrange a short nightly Epilogue in its commercial break after *News at Ten* so that the news of the day be given a Christian comment and that flaming passions, burning buildings and petrol bombs could be mollified by Christian compassion.[32]

The vanguardist thrust of RTE in the south has probably caused more controversy over the years than its equivalent has done in the north.[33] At least for BBC NI and UTV, there is the security of the larger British institutions to fall back on – RTE is more exposed.

One of the Catholic Hierarchy's more sophisticated analysts, the Bishop of Clogher, Dr. Joseph Duffy, said recently:

> If the media does not reflect the underlying Christian values of our society, then the Church will continue to decline and the quality of life will continue to suffer . . . Journalists have to try to analyse in Christian terms . . . Very often one gets the impression that in the analysis one leaves the Christianity in your private compartment, and does the analysis along some other lines (sic) [34]

The 'some other lines' which the journalist pursues are the liberal humanist values implicit in public service broadcasting. Impartiality and balance will ensure that the church, as a powerful social and political, as well as religious, institution will not be above scrutiny, analysis, comment or criticism. When the Catholic Church, institutionally, demands that there be no distinction between moral matters and political matters, as it did in the case of the referenda in the 1980s, it cannot be surprised when the same journalistic standards which apply in relation to other political opinion, is applied to it. The public service ethos cannot countenance, as Bishop Duffy implies, that either 'Christian' values in Ireland be equated with the institutional authority of the Church, or that the Church be somehow above criticism, even from committed Christian journalists.

RTE, of course, runs a gauntlet of pressure – on one hand from a government tradition which cannot always see the distinction between the interests of the government and the interests of the state and a Church which refuses to make the distinction between its institutional interests and those of the state, something which is taken for granted in other liberal democracies. The twin pressures of God and Caesar have visited many controversies on RTE over the years.[35]

I have spent some time teasing out the problems, as I see them, of broadcasting's vanguardist role in Ireland, using *Inside Ulster* as an example. But the hegemonic thrust of 'the big We' is not the only strategy which is available. I want now to turn to the potential which exists for a different, more radical strategy, one which is

more adequate to the complexity of cultural identity seen as a
dynamic process rather than a static condition. And I want to
argue that this potential is released, and realised, where the local
meets the global.

4. Inventions and Re-imaginings

It is not in the mere negation of existing social perceptions that
different forces can be generated. It is in two positive and
connected initiatives: first the cultural struggle for actual social
identities; and second, the political definition of effective self-
governing societies.[36]

Raymond Williams has proposed these initiatives as the way
forward towards a new millennium, in an intricate and at times
provocative analysis of what he has dubbed 'the culture of nations'. At the heart of these two initiatives there lies a concern for
the real, face-to-face sense of community which has long since
disappeared under Anderson's 'imagined community' of the nation (with all of its symbolic trappings of flags, emblems, monar-
chy and 'national' interest) and swamped by the centralised power
of state bureaucracy. Indeed Williams goes on to argue:

It is now very apparent, in the development of modern industrial societies, that the nation-state, in its classical European
forms, is at once too large and too small for the range of real
social purposes. It is too large, even in the old nation-states such
as Britain, to develop full social identities in their real diversity.[37]

It is too small, he continues, to deal with the truly frightening
scale of the problems which confront, not just the peoples within
nation states, but the human race in general – ie the real global
problems of world poverty, the environment, wars or the danger
of nuclear annihilation.
    In other words, Williams here proposes a new negotiation be-
tween the local and the global – one which decentres power within
the old nation states and empowers people within their own social
identities or actual human communities. At the same time connections are made both within and across previous nation states to
similarly empowered social identities 'in their real diversity'.
    Williams was writing in the early 1980s and died before the great

upheavals in Eastern Europe in 1989 brought into clearer focus
this relationship between local, national and global perspectives.
But he anticipated one central element in what was to follow these
upheavals – a re-awakening of interest in questions of ethnic and
national identity. Indeed, as the years have progressed, the debates over European integration and its impact on established
notions of identity have become central to political discourse
throughout the continent.

And nowhere more so than in Ireland. It is hardly surprising
that the continuing banalities and tragedies of the conflict in
Ireland should be inserted into the European debate. Possible
solutions, uncannily resembling Williams' dual initiatives, are now
being fulsomely canvassed within a European context.[38]

Now I think it is important and necessary to accord the notion
of Europe or European identity, especially when seen as a panacea
for all our problems, with a degree of healthy scepticism, as Philip
Schlesinger does below.[39] 'Europe' is no more a given than the
nation is – 'European identity' no less an artefact than national
identity. If we are to realise a changed relationship within Europe
then it must be the result of 'initiative', 'cultural struggle' and
'political definition', as Williams has argued. It must be worked for
– our social identities and political relationships must be *re-imagined*, in other words.

But I believe the potential is there, and believe with Williams
that the key to this is the empowerment of communities away from
the centre. Obviously it would be to exacerbate the problem
merely to centralise all power – political, economic or cultural – in
a supranational structure and then attempt a hegemonic 'big We'
called 'European identity'. Rather, as Neal Ascherson has argued.

It is fair to conclude, . . . that the process of European integration means that the nation-state is leaking power both upwards
to Brussels and downwards to regional level. Within the new
outer shell of the integrated Community, the tough skin of the
old nation-states will grow swiftly permeable and porous. The
cultural and political components which will become the real
units of this Europe, acquiring definition rather than losing it,
will be the regions.[40]

This investment in the notion of a 'Europe of the regions' is a
key political goal and the prospects for successfully re-imagining

our identity rests upon its eventually coming about. There are, no doubt, very considerable difficulties ahead. Richard Kearney for example has pointed to the ironic fact that the UK and Ireland are today, the two most centralised states in the EC, both with very poor records in regard to empowering local communities.[41] But the process of integration is well underway, and the global nature of contemporary finance capital means that there is little choice available to formerly sovereign nation-states. It is not a philosophical question of 'is this the right thing to do?' – it is a practical question of 'yes, but on what terms and in whose interest and through what structures?' It is, therefore a *political* issue requiring new inventions, re-imaginings, different artefacts which are more liberating and not even more debilitating than the ones which we already have.

If it is a political issue at one level, is has profound cultural implications at an even deeper one. Already, the search for other cultural definitions has begun. In local terms, one can cite the excavation of (temporarily) forgotten writers, like John Hewitt or Sam Hanna Bell, or John Wilson Foster's notion of a 'radical regionalism'. [42]

And in more global terms, Kenneth Frampton, in a very influential essay, promotes the notion of a 'critical regionalism' in regard to architecture, but one which has been appropriated much more widely in regard to culture in general. Frampton argues in favour of what he calls an 'arrière-garde'.

> It is my contention that only an arrière-garde has the capacity to cultivate a resistant, identity – giving culture while at the same time having discreet recourse to universal technique . . . The fundamental strategy of Critical Regionalism is to mediate the impact of universal civilization with elements derived *indirectly* from the peculiarities of a particular place. It is clear . . . that Critical Regionalism depends upon maintaining a high level of critical self-consciousness. It may find its governing inspiration in such things as the range and quality of the local light, or in a *tectonic* derived from a peculiar structural mode, or in the topography of a given site.[43]

The local light, the sense of place or 'rootedness' as Williams calls it, is a check against the homogenising tendency in universal culture, the blockage against more repressive formulations of a bigger and then an even bigger, 'We'. It can be seen here, that the implication is again to release *local* creative energies and further-more that this be done in a critically reflective manner. In broad-casting terms this means not only empowering local communities to represent themselves, to have a voice and a visibility of them-selves, but that this should happen through an exploration of the diverse factors which constitute those communities' identities.

Now this has profound implications for what we might under-stand as a *national* broadcasting service (and indeed what we might understand as a *national* cinema). The key component here is the looming presence of American film and television culture – the threat of the 'Los Angelesation' of the world's audio-visual culture. This is no recent threat, of course.

American cinema has dominated the world's screens since the First World War and the sheer economic muscle of the American television industry has ensured that the world's television screens have been awash with American imports since at least the early 1960s. The problem has been 1) how to gauge the effect of this and 2) how to deal with it.

In many European states, policy was directed at establishing quotas of imported to indigenous production, encouraging in particular the notion of a *national* culture as a response to the homogenising effects of the *international*. But there were two fun-damental problems here. First, as many critics have noted, Ameri-can culture was popular with different national audiences not only because the American culture industries had the economic mus-cle to penetrate foreign markets, but because American popular culture offered real pleasures to national audiences everywhere.[44] Second, the type of *national* response encouraged by the nation states tended to promote a narrow, elitist form of culture which did not reflect the real social communities in their diversity, or reflect their needs and aspirations. In a discussion on British national cinema, John Hill quotes Geoffrey Nowell-Smith's con-tention that, when compared to American films, British cinema appeared 'restrictive and stifling, subservient to middle-class artis-tic models and to middle and upper-class values'.[45] It is hardly surprising in these circumstances, that the classless, democratic appeal of American popular culture would appear positively liber-ating.

Similarly in Ireland. It is equally unsurprising that Irish audi-ences should so willingly embrace the cultural products of America from within a stifling, conservative (and heavily censored) official national culture. Indeed much of the censorship in Ireland down to the 1960s was directed precisely at popular cultural forms – the cinema, comics, magazines, popular literature and even popular dance and music. The following comment from a contributor to the *Irish Radio Review* in 1927 makes uneasy reading for a contemporary sensibility but it accurately reflects the thrust of a lot of official national hostility in these years to American popular culture (and echoes, indeed, Walsh's 'British music-hall dope').

I know that my feet will begin to tap the floor if I hear a Jazz-band strike up a tune. I know that the natural instinct is for me to move my body in all sorts of ridiculous ways that my ancestors discarded thousands of years ago . . . But I ask, is that all that Jazz can do? Can it not awake other than animal instincts in me? Has it not other than 'nigger' qualities. I, for one do not want to ape the nigger. I wonder if all those people who profess to go into an ecstasy when they hear the *haunting* strains of the 'Hoola-Hoola-Blues', or such-like clap-trap, know that it is nothing short of a reversal to the primitive, when they allow themselves to be carried away by such arrant nonsense.[46]

But, of course, popular audiences were quite content, throughout Europe, to allow themselves to be carried away by the rhythms and images of American popular culture. Indeed, the influence of this culture now forms an important element in the rich complexities of European cultural identities and it is this fact which makes Frampton's notion of a critical regionalism, where the local indigenous meets the universal, so attractive. In bringing this about the narrowness of the official nationalism sponsored by the nation-states themselves, is as much of a problem as is the homogenising impulses of global American culture. Hence the importance, in line with the previously discussed political goal, of empowering the local to create its own audio-visual culture.

The challenge, then, is quite clear. It is not to surrender abjectly to the universal culture delivered by market forces, nor to pursue a national essence through narrow and restrictive policy, but to seek out a third way, contingent upon releasing the submerged experiences of diverse social communities. What then are the prospects, in relation to broadcasting and film, for this third way?

Some of the necessary pre-conditions already exist. First, it must now be acknowledged that the capacity of nation states to control incoming culture has been irrevocably eroded. As we have seen, nationally constituted audiences have already contributed to this through choice and predilection. In addition, new technological developments, especially in cable and satellite, have effectively eroded the nation-state's capacity to patrol the airwaves (though it is often forgotten that this erosion happened much earlier in regard to radio broadcasting).

Second, and more crucially, the old nation-state broadcasting systems have already begun to decentralise – in Britain and to a lesser extent in Ireland, through the deregulation policies of market-orientated governments. This is an ironic, but nonetheless welcome, side-effect of the current onslaught on public service broadcasting, one that was presaged earlier by the commissioning framework of Channel Four. As more and more television production is commissioned from independent producers, the potential exists for this third way, this critical regionalism to develop.

Rod Stoneman below indicates one of the advantages of this. Independent production can sometimes approach issues from a slightly different or oblique angle than can the centralised production of the big institutions. Independent producers often have a more finely-tuned sense of a community or the issues which emanate from a particular region. More importantly though, this decentralisation can allow for funding to be diverted to more specifically community or regional-based independents, allowing them access eventually to the airwaves.

Third, an important development from the European Commission provides the possibility of supranational support for regional audio-visual production, surely a central requirement if this third way is to develop properly. Originally set up in 1985, the MEDIA 92 initiative was established to prepare the European industry for the greater demands of the Single Market in 1992. As the pilot programme proceeded, the cultural dimensions of the initiative became more focused, although the tension between the demands of 'industry' and the claims for 'culture' remain. The implications of this tension have been commented on by Roberto Barzanti, President of the European Parliament Commission for both Media and Culture.

Preserving the dozens of cultures which make up Europe and gaining, at the same time, the necessary competitiveness at world level . . . this is the problem to be solved if European artistic creativity and freedom of expression itself is to survive the Single Market and 'deregulation'. The American production and distribution model is best suited to the Single Market economy . . . Should we, then, imitate the American model? As far as Europe is concerned there is no question of this . . . Europe must retain its separate identities while at the same time developing its 'culture industry' . . . The choice had to be made but let there be no mistaking the fact that it will be extremely costly, too.[47]

Now constituted under the title of MEDIA, the initiative supports twelve different pilot projects with a budget over the next four years of ECU250 million. Barzanti has indicated that to be successful a lot more money than this will be needed. Nonetheless, it remains a hopeful development and even at its pilot stage, it offers considerable opportunities for broadcasters and independent producers in Ireland. Among the twelve pilot programmes, there are initiatives on film and video distribution – the European Film and Distribution Office (EFDO) and Espace Video European (EVE, administered by the Irish Film Institute in Dublin) – and on production and training – European Script award (SCRIPT) and Les Entrepreneurs de l'Audiovisuel Europeen (EAVE).

Among the new initiatives outlined for MEDIA over the next four years, the following have obvious interest for Irish broadcasters and independent producers:

- Encouragement of TV networks to broadcast programmes produced by independent European producers
- Support for the development of multilingual TV channels
- Incentive to set up and develop structures liable to mobilise and stimulate investment.
- The development of potential in the countries and regions with restricted audiovisual capacity and in minority language regions of the Community.
- Support for original documentaries.[48]

These initiatives, like all European initiatives, need political support. It seems to me then, again echoing Rod Stoneman's opinion below, that in Ireland both the broadcasters and the independent producers within the regions, need to organise more effectively in support of the 'cultural' dimensions of these 'industry' initiatives.

7   The phrase is Winston Churchill's, quoted in A.T.Q. Stewart, *The Narrow Ground: The Roots of Conflict in Ulster*, London, Faber, 1977
8   For a summary overview of these approaches, see Philip Schlesinger, *Media, State and Nation*, London, Sage Publications, 1991
9   Benedict Anderson, *Imagined Communities*, London, Verso, 1983
10 Martin McLoone, 'Lear's Fool and Goya's Dilemma', in *Circa*, No 50, Mar/Apr 1990
11 Ibid for a brief discussion of this relationship in the Irish context .
12 Eric Hobsbawm and Terence Ranger (eds), *The Invention of Tradition*, Cambridge, 1983
13 Roland Barthes, *Mythologies*, London, Paladin, 1973
14 *The Irish Radio Review*, Vol 3, No 1, Oct 1927
15 Anderson, op.cit.
16 Ibid
17 David Cardiff and Paddy Scannell, 'Broadcasting and national unity' in James Curran et al (eds), *Impacts and Influences*, London, Methuen, 1987
18 See Stuart Hall, Ian Connell and Lidia Curti, 'The Unity of Current Affairs Television', in Tony Bennett et al (eds), *Popular Television and Film*, London, BFI, 1981
19 Cardiff and Scannell op cit.
20 David Butler, 'Ulster Unionism and British Broadcasting Journalism 1924–89' in Bill Rolston (ed), *The Media and Northern Ireland: Covering the Troubles*, London, Macmillan, 1991. See also Rex Cathcart, *The Most Contrary Region: The BBC in Northern Ireland 1924–84*, Belfast, Blackstaff, 1984.
21 Butler, op.cit.
22 Asa Briggs, *The History of Broadcasting in the United Kingdom*, Vol 1, Oxford, OUP, 1961
23 Dail Debates, Vol 103, col 484
24 Luke Gibbons, 'From Megalith to Megastore: Broadcasting and Irish Culture', in Thomas Bartlett et al (eds), *Irish Studies: A general introduction*, Dublin, Gill and MacMillan, 1988
25 For a discussion of RTE's role in Irish society see Martin McLoone and John MacMahon (eds), *Television and Irish Society*, Dublin, RTE/IFI, 1984
26 Raymond Williams, *Television: Technology and Cultural Form*, Glasgow, Fontana, 1974
27 Butler op.cit., Cathcart, op.cit.
28 Gorham, op.cit.
29 Described in Asa Briggs, *The BBC: the First Fifty Years*, Oxford, OUP, 1985
30 Butler, op.cit.
31 See for instance some of the comments on the programme in Maurna Crozier(ed), *Cultural Traditions in Northern Ireland: Varieties of Irishness*, Belfast, Institute of Irish Studies, 1989, p 101
32 Brum Henderson, *A Musing on the Lighter Side of Ulster Television and its First 25 Years*, Belfast, UTV Publications, 1984
33 See for example Gorham op.cit; McLoone and MacMahon op.cit. and Muris MacConghail, 'The Creation of RTE and the Impact of Television' in Brian Farrell (ed), *Communications and Community in Ireland*, Dublin, Mercier Press/RTE 1984
34 *The Sunday Tribune*, 17th February 1991
35 For a discussion of the political pressures see Mary Kelly, 'Twenty Years of Current Affairs on RTE' in McLoone and MacMahon op.cit. Also

MacConghail op.cit. For a discussion of the religious pressures see Maurice Earls, 'The Late Late Show – Controversy and Context' in McLoone and MacMahon op.cit.

36 Raymond Williams, *Towards 2000*, Harmondsworth, Pelican, 1985

37 Ibid

38 See, for example, many of the contributors in Richard Kearney (ed), *Across the Frontiers*, Dublin, Wolfhound Press, 1988 and Maurna Crozier (ed), *Cultural Traditions in Northern Ireland: All Europeans Now?*, Belfast, Institute of Irish Studies, 1991

39 See also George Watson, 'All Europeans Now?' in Crozier op.cit (1991)

40 Neal Ascherson, 'Europe of the Regions' in Crozier (ed) op.cit. (1991)

41 Richard Kearney, 'Across the Frontiers : Ireland and Europe', in Crozier (ed) op.cit. (1991)

42 John Wilson Foster, 'Radical Regionalism', in *The Irish Review*, No 7, Autumn 1989

43 Kenneth Frampton, 'Towards a Critical Regionalism: Six Points for an Architecture of Resistance', in Hal Foster (ed) *Postmodern Culture*, London, Pluto Press, 1985

44 See for example Duncan Webster, *Looka Yonder: The Imaginary America of Populist Culture*, London, Routledge, 1989

45 John Hill, 'The Issue of National Cinema and British Film Production' in Duncan Petrie (ed), *BFI Working Papers Vol 1: New Questions of British Cinema*, London, BFI, forthcoming.

46 AZ, 'The Listening Post', in *Irish Radio Review*, Vol 3, No 1, Oct 1927

47 *MEDIA 92 : Newsletter of the MEDIA 92 Programme*, No 6, Sept 1990

48 Ibid

49 M McLoone, 'Lear's Fool, Goya's Dilemma', op.cit.

PART II

CULTURE, IDENTITY AND BROADCASTING IN IRELAND

Local Issues, Global Perspectives

Proceedings of the Cultural Traditions Group/Media Studies,
UUC Symposium, 21st February, 1991

WELCOMING ADDRESS

Professor Robert Welch

Head of Department English Media and Theatre Studies

Friends, colleagues and visitors to the University, I want to welcome all of you to the Coleraine campus of the University of Ulster for this forum on Cultural Identity and Broadcasting in Ireland. The fact that there has been such interest in this forum reflected in the turnout this morning from the academic world, north and south of the border, from across the water and also, of course, most importantly the practising media people themselves, means that this kind of conference is most welcome, long overdue perhaps, but crucially providing an opportunity for academics and practising media people to get together and talk about the thing that preoccupies them most: the nature of broadcasting, what it reflects, how it may be interrogated, how it may be thought about, what are the opportunities for research, development and thought.

We know how important the image is, whether the broadcast image or the reproduced image. We are aware of the great wealth of information, verbal or visual that comes at us from all sides these days. It is most important that academics and broadcast people get together and have the opportunity to think about values and ethical concerns, to think about those things that govern the nature of the media, and how images and information come at us, how we may think about them, and indeed question them. There is also perhaps something special too about holding a symposium in this particular place. This University and the Media Studies section in our department occupies a unique place in the broadcasting culture of these islands, situated, as it is, between two very powerful modes of representation and transmission, the British and the Irish. We know the force of the media, and we know, too, our responsibility to reflect upon its role in the interaction between Ireland and England, which is I suppose at its most intense in this part of the world, in Northern Ireland. So I wish the proceedings well, I know that you will have a fruitful and engaging day. Thank you very much.

INTRODUCTION TO SYMPOSIUM

Martin McLoone

Lecturer in Media Studies, UUC

Symposium Organiser

As Professor Welch has indicated, we are slightly overwhelmed by the response to this symposium, which is why we delayed the start for fifteen minutes or so. A lot of people have now arrived but I think a lot more are yet to come, travelling from Derry, Belfast, Dublin and other places. So, let me reiterate and welcome you all this morning and beg your indulgence for the slight delay in getting underway.

Of course, in another sense, I suppose we should not be surprised that a discussion like this should touch a nerve with so many people. These are exciting times and changing times, for the two broad issues which, today, we set out to explore – broadcasting and its relationship to notions of identity.

What I want to do now is to place the symposium in some kind of context for you, to explain what I had in mind when putting it together in this precise manner and finally indicate what I hope will come out of our discussions by the end of the day.

As I indicated in the advance publicity for this symposium, our primary focus is on the relationship between broadcasting, (defined as it is today, to include the work of independent producers as well as in-house productions) and the question of identity in Ireland. However, there are two broad contexts in which we want to place these discussions and it is these contexts which interest us in the sessions this morning.

First of all we want to consider the amazingly rapid and far reaching changes that have taken place in Eastern Europe in the last two years or so. The collapse of the old communist regimes has given rise again to questions relating to nationalism, to national identity and ethnic consciousness throughout Eastern Europe. We are also witnessing an unfortunate consequence of this, which maybe touches a particular nerve with us in Ireland – the re-emergence of ethnic conflict and intercommunal strife.

On the other hand, though, from January 1st 1992, economically at least, things will not be the same for the twelve members of the European Community, as we enter the Single Market. Undoubtedly this will also have enormous implications for all areas of social and cultural life. As one part of Europe disintegrates, our part of Europe attempts greater integration and we want to keep at the back of our minds the implications of all this when we discuss the problems about identity in Ireland itself.

The second, complex set of changes which are at the back of our minds when we talk about Ireland and broadcasting relates to broadcasting itself. We are now well down the road in the development of cable and satellite technologies. We are well down the road in a process of deregulation of the old broadcast systems which operated in Europe for more or less forty years since the end of the Second World War. In Britain and in Ireland we are facing a period when new broadcasting legislation is actually changing the system of broadcasting that we have been so used to.

These macro changes in the social and economic sphere, and the micro changes in terms of one set of technologies, have implications for the cultural issues which we want to address here today – the question of culture and identity as it specifically manifests itself in an Ireland which is totally part of the European Community, whilst at the same time is internally divided between the part which is an independent nation-state and that which is within the United Kingdom. There is, then, a sense of complexity about all this which has enormous implications for the way in which we might think about broadcasting and cultural traditions in Ireland.

Now I want to slip if I may, into a slightly autobiographical note, to explain why this symposium has taken the shape that is has. I have been influenced by two professional experiences over the last year or so. I want to refer, first of all, to my experiences in April, 1990, when I was on the international jury at the eleventh Celtic Film Festival, held in Gweedore. I'm sure many of you here today also attended that event.

This proved to be an enormously illuminating experience, I must say. Over a period of four days, the jury saw a range of films and programmes from Ireland (north and south), Scotland, Wales, Brittany and Cornwall. These represented all levels of the produc-

tion process, from the well-funded (or relatively well-funded) productions of the broadcasting institutions right through to the first-
time films or videos of students. We saw a range of films that were
in the dominant languages of English or French, as well as those in
the various minority languages – Irish, Scots-Gallic, Welsh, Breton
and even Cornish.

Seeing these films in a concentrated period, I was able to detect
two strands into which this film and programme making seemed
to fall. I found this an interesting perspective from which to judge
how film makers in all of these countries actually tried to negotiate
the question of identity.

The first strand of film making I would characterise as basically
nostalgic in mood. These films tended to look back to a period of
time in the past when the cultural identity of that specific nation
(be it the Irish, the Welsh or whatever) seemed clearer, more
specific, more tangible and less blurred than it would appear
today. The films celebrated, or lamented, a way of life, a mode of
production, which had changed irrevocably. A sense of national
identity, or national pride, was sought in the past, rather than in
the present, and inevitably these films tended to reflect a rather
sorrowful, nostalgic mood.

The second strand of film making was much more contemporary and much more exploratory, sometimes even a bit experi-
mental in form. These were, in many instances, much less well-
rounded and less well-accomplished as finished productions but
none the less interesting for the way in which they tried to explore
identity as a set of contemporary contradictions. Identity in these
films was not a given but was a complex of different influences,
different attitudes, constantly changing, constantly open to movement and re-thinking.

Now my own predilection was for that second mode of film
making – the more exploratory approach – simply because it
raised identity not as a given, but as a problem, which I think
identity is. That's not to say that the other type of production did
not have its points of interest. But I want to raise the possibility
here, and maybe leave it for people to come back to during the
day, that these films represent two ways of trying to negotiate the
whole question of identity. On one hand, you can look for some
essential fact, or essential moment in your identity, or seek out an
essence and try to freeze it or fix it. Or you can propose a sense of
identity which is contradictory, many-layered, confused and con-

fusing – a kind of contemporary sense of identity in flux. I, at least, came away from Gweedore with a desire to see more films and programmes which pursued identity in its fluidity rather than in its supposed essence.

The second experience, I suppose, which has moulded the way in which I have thought about this symposium, stems from the fact that for the last year or so, I have been a member of the Media Group of the Cultural Traditions Group. The media group is charged with the daunting task of giving money away to film makers and broadcasters. The key stipulation for giving that money away is that the films, programmes or videos that will subsequently be made will somehow explore cultural tradition, or cultural traditions, in Ireland.

Now it seems to me that that is easier said than done. We have a key stipulation, but what does, or should, guide our decisions? What kinds of films should we support? Is there some way in which we can copperfasten our criteria? After all, that key stipulation is a rather broad one. Can you here – as the broadcasters, the film makers, the video producers, the academics, the educationalists, the community workers and so on – can you advise us what we should be doing with this money?

Now I'm sure you will agree with me, that this is a rather nice position for the media group to be in. It's not a lot of money, certainly, in broadcasting terms, in film making terms, but it is more money than anybody else is giving away at the moment for film and video production.

What this does allow us to do today, I hope, is to move beyond a concentration on questions of funding. Now I don't want to imply that these questions are unimportant – they are, of course, very important. However, one other observation I made at the Celtic Film Festival was that, despite how interesting those forty or so films were, from the different Celtic countries, those films did not form the focus of discussion at the festival. I was particularly disappointed that nobody seemed to want to discuss the films that *had* been made, and maybe draw some lessons from these, but rather they wanted to discuss how they might make their *next* film in terms of the funding and financing thereof.

Now this is, of course, understandable. But I have always thought that an equally crucial question is, if the money is in place, what kinds of films should we make, or ought we to make? I suppose then, that having the Cultural Traditions Group funding policy at the back of what we are discussing today, it might allow us to go beyond the question of funding to consider what kinds of films, t.v. programmes and videos we might aspire to make. If anything sums up where I would hope we get to by the end of the day, it is precisely to that kind of discussion.

And equally, it seems to me that if one wants to make films in the future, it helps to know what has been done in the past, is being done at present, both here and elsewhere and to draw out implications or lessons that might be learnt. So perhaps throughout the day we might make reference to these and indeed we might also consider programming policies and strategies – broadcast performance – in Ireland, north and south.

We might consider, for example, the ways in which RTE has dealt with the cultural traditions of Northern Ireland. Has RTE tried successfully in the past, does it try now, to explain Protestant Unionist culture in the North to its own audience? To what extent have the BBC or UTV been successful in representing the different cultural traditions of Northern Ireland or indeed in explaining to their Northern Ireland audiences just what the cultural traditions of the South are? How successfully have all three facilitated the kind of internal exploration of cultural contradiction which I referred to earlier?

In other words, I am proposing a wide-ranging interrogation of the film making of the past within the larger contexts I have talked about, all coming together (I am a great optimist) at the end to discuss our aspirations for the future.

A couple of things about the symposium itself, before I move on. You will have noticed, I have no doubt, a gap in the listing of speakers for our second session this morning. Originally Robin Walsh, the Controller of BBC NI had agreed to speak at that session but to his horror, and my great disappointment, he later discovered that the date clashes with a broadcasting council meeting. I had to do a quick tippex job on the programme running order! There is not, therefore, an 'official' BBC voice, as it were, in that spot. These things happen when an event like this is organised at such short notice.

Having said that, though, there are lots of BBC people here today, who will, no doubt, join our discussions in an unofficial capacity, so to speak. In the afternoon session, of course, Michael McGowan, from BBC Radio Foyle, will address us on the question of broadcasting in a divided community.

I am delighted to say, however, that if we have lost one important guest, we have gained another, who is not listed on your
programme. Rod Stoneman, who is a commissioning editor for
Channel Four, is with us and has very generously agreed to speak
at short notice in the second session. I am very grateful to him, and
to all our listed speakers, for agreeing to come along today.

Having said all this, there is one final point which I want to stress
anyway. I never have envisaged the situation between the speakers
up here on the platform and you the audience on the floor, as a
teaching situation, where you are being told something which you
don't know. That is obviously ridiculous since about fifty of you
could easily be 'on the platform'.

The day has been planned as a kind of open forum, where
certain people have agreed to give stimulating ten minute talks
and then to throw open the discussion to the general body of
people here. If one could re-draw the geography of this lecture
theatre, I suppose I am trying to imagine us all at a rather large
round table (the serried ranks of the seating here is perhaps one
example of how form can sometimes dictate content!) The lecture
theatre ambience is not what I have in mind – we are all in this
together!

OK, then – the one slight deviation from the format of the day is
that I have asked Professor Philip Schlesinger to take twenty-five
minutes or so, to enlarge on those European issues which I mentioned earlier. Philip Schlesinger's session will be chaired by James
Hawthorne, Chairman of the Community Relations Council (our
sponsors for the day) and a man who in the past has worn a
number of hats not unconnected with broadcasting. Thank you all
for coming, we welcome you Jimmy, and I hand over to Jimmy
Hawthorne to get the symposium proper underway. Thank you.

SESSION 1

Chair: James Hawthorne

Chairman Community Relations Council

Global Perspectives

At a time when the whole world seems to be indulging in the ultimate video game from the Gulf, there might be some expectation for me to attempt to say something resonant about the role and power of the media and in particular the broadcasting media. But we who live on this island, and in this part of the island, have already assessed that power and after years of the hard story, the graphic film, the investigative journalism, the truncated interview and the studio discussion, perhaps we might agree with the the the remark of the great French Cubist painter Henri Matisse when he said 'Exactitude is not necessarily the truth'. Perhaps it will be the work of the imagination – drama for example – and not news and current affairs, which may get closer to that truth but I believe that there are many other forms of broadcasting, yet to be invented, which will increase an understanding of ourselves.

Our thinking has been turning to the potential of media to define our true identity, to increase our confidence but not our certainties, to expose some useful doubts, perhaps to spring some nice surprises but above all to clear our minds and enlarge our horizons and perhaps generate some long over due optimism and a firmer resolve to tackle our own problems.

Philip Schlesinger is Professor of Film and Media Studies at the University of Stirling. He has published extensively in the area of cultural identity and nationalism with particular concern for minority cultures in Europe. To students of media he is perhaps best known for his now classic academic study on BBC news-gathering *Putting 'Reality' Together* [1] which, for many of you in this audience, has been prescribed reading. Within the BBC, there was not, I confess, the same degree of collective eagerness to embrace his findings but, if it was not *pre*scribed there is no evidence to suggest that it was actually *pro*scribed. He's also co-author of an equally influential study on political violence *Televising Terrorism* [2].

We are delighted to secure his interest in our symposium and delighted that he agreed to give this opening keynote lecture.

NOTES

1 Philip Schlesinger, *Putting 'Reality' Together : BBC News*, London, Constable, 1978.
2 Philip Schlesinger, Graham Murdock, Philip Elliot, *Televising 'Terrorism'*, London, Comedia, 1983.

COLLECTIVE IDENTITIES IN A CHANGING EUROPE

Philip Schlesinger

Professor of Film and Media Studies, University of Stirling

Thank you for the introduction. I began to feel the introductions were getting interminable and if there is any one else here who would like to be introduced please let me know.

When I agreed to come along to this meeting I was told that it was going to be a small intimate seminar. 'There is this nice "Provencale" restaurant near Bushmills. Just come along, write a few things down on the back of an envelope, and we will gather a dozen people around a table and have a chat and stimulate a little discussion.' Since I agreed to that particular set of terms of reference the game changed and I have come hot from my lap top computer this morning with a written text. This has a number of key words in it which I am obliged to present to you: so it's not a matter of extemporizing. I have actually written something and I am now going to read it.

The Cultural Traditions Group has begun a valuable discussion about dimensions of Irishness and of Britishness. Although not directly part of that developing tradition of debate, this particular symposium is clearly close kin to it. The other progenitors of today's event, my colleagues in Media Studies, at Coleraine, have also been active in developing work on questions of national and cultural identity. As we have readily agreed in our previous discussions, it is no accident that these interests are increasingly at the centre of media studies in the Celtic countries.

I have been asked to take the argument one step further and move outside the confines of these peripheral islands to talk about 'European-ness' and its implications for our identities. This is a tall order; but I shall do my best to share my thinking with you. It is certainly a theme that I have been considering quite consistently since the mid-1980s. I shall explain how this came about in a moment.

Before I go on to this, I should like to pay tribute to your initiative in creating this framework for reflection and debate. Naturally, it owes a great deal to the existence of the complex communal differences and the related conflicts that have marked Northern Ireland. But to seek to explore diversity in a spirit of tolerance is a value close to my heart. In fact, it is really at the basis of all I have to say today.

I was particularly struck by the fact that we are participating in a forum one of whose key words is 'culture'. Back on the other island, and outside rather restricted academic and intellectual circles, it seems to me that 'culture' is not a term much used. For instance I think that when people were talking about Glasgow being the European City of Culture 1990, it was always with a slight incredulity . The arts, education, the media, sport, the so called heritage industries, are somehow regarded as institutions in their own right, and not, in the normal course of events, conceived of as articulated with one another, or as components of a national culture or cultures. I am much more familiar with the concept of 'culture' as a way of framing discussion about broadcasting in Latin Europe (which my Mediterranean soul repeatedly drives me to visit) than in the so-called Anglo-Saxon world. In similar vein, if you can say the word 'intellectual' and keep a straight face you must be on the continent. To judge by the inscrutability all around me, in addressing this symposium I could rightly imagine myself to be in Montpellier, Bologna or Barcelona, aside from the weather. Perhaps that already tells us quite a lot about Irish European-ness.

Speaking of Ireland, I have never had anything but pleasure or a variety of stimulating experiences from my visits here, whether north or south of the border, so of course I am delighted to be present at this gathering and honoured to be asked. I should add that I have had a long-standing interest in this island, perhaps due to the good fortune of an education that left me with at least a sense of the importance of Ireland's place in any history of Britain and also of Britain's responsibilities for the present-day shape of things over here. By a quirk of fate, already referred to I think, my doctoral research into broadcast journalism at the beginning of the 1970s could hardly allow me to ignore the impact of the troubles on the propaganda war, since then waged without end. Questions of political violence and questions of communication have been indissociable for me since the outset of my academic career, and this perception has left an enduring mark upon much of my subsequent work.

But that is really by the way, for today, thank goodness, I am not obliged to dwell on censorship and political conflict, which is a pleasant change. Actually, although the topic of identity in Europe is apparently much less controversial, I am not at all sure that it will long remain so. In the near future, when we talk about Europe's multifold identities, shall we not also often be talking about political violence waged between states and those collectivities who do not wish to be their citizens? Witness, for instance, the Soviet state's repression taking place in the Baltic republics at present – and that is only one example. The political role of the media of communication, not least of broadcasting, in the struggles between central state machineries and national groups seeking autonomy or separatism, is, I regret, going to be on our agenda continuously during the decade to come. Programme-makers will not be able to avoid this. Indeed, they are already producing a good deal on this theme.

Let me move on, however, to talk more directly about the question of identity in Europe. My interest was first seriously aroused, and if you believe this you will believe anything, when working at the European University Institute, housed in the Badia Fiesolana, a former abbey which overlooks Florence – one is tempted to add, sounding the appropriate note of touristic kitsch, that incomparable gem of European civilisation. In this idyllic setting (replete with plots and sub-plots enough to keep Umberto Eco busy on a further large work of fiction) there was a great deal of integrationist Euro-babble (the official ideology), alongside a painstaking and precise division of academic and administrative jobs by nationality. The German-speaking world calls it *Proporz* and the Italians call *Lottizzazione,* we might simply call it a carve up. Amongst this Tuscan-based Euro-community of scholars, English dominated as the language of instruction, French was the pre-eminent language of the bureaucracy, Italian absolutely indispensable for the mensa. There was also a silent language, weighed down into reticence by an historical guilt – this was in 1985-86 – namely, German. I imagine that today it has found its voice. Indeed, I hope so. As a flawed attempt at producing a Euro-intelligentsia, this was certainly an interesting set-up. However, to my eye at least, what was particularly striking was how what we loosely call national character tended to persist in one's everyday dealings.

As will be obvious, the point of this tale is to sound a personal note of caution about facile ideas of easily creating a 'European identity' and to take a certain distance from the seductive promise that such ideas are supposed to contain – not least to underline, from the start, my view that the present anchorage points of statehood and nationhood (a very important distinction there as everyone will appreciate) will not cease to be highly relevant for the foreseeable future.

How should we begin to discuss Europe and identity today?

Let me initially consider some of the general issues that arise when we talk about identities. In our present context, we are concerned with the ways in which collectivities construct, and continually reconstruct, a sense of themselves by reference to the signs provided by cultures. Such collectivities can take quite varied shapes: nations, ethnic groups, religious confessions, political movements would all be examples. For our purpose, the central interest lies in the ill-defined categories of national and cultural identities.

If we take one step back, and try quite abstractly to delineate some of the features of collective identities, I believe that we need to consider the following. First, the making of identities is an *active process*. We are what we are not because of any essence lurking within us but because of how we as a group have evolved and interrelate to other groups. To put it slightly differently, to belong to a collectivity involves a process of inclusion, a grouping of oneself with those who are like 'us'. There is also a process of exclusion, of defining 'them', those who are 'not-us' (in various gradations) as different, as outsiders, as aliens, as a threat, at the extreme, as inhuman and eliminable.

Second, we need to be aware of the temporal dimension through which the highly complex imaginary process of creating traditions and of activating collective memories occurs. I refer for instance to the battles remembered, the heroes and heroines cherished, the language, images and stories transmitted through the generations, the foes inherited: if you like, to 'our' version of history, or perhaps more correctly to 'our' mythology. Collective remembrance necessarily also involves selective amnesia, for in casting a certain light upon the past we also throw much of it into shadow.

Third, we also need to think spatially. The primordial attachment of a collectivity is often to a particular land or territory. But it need not always conform to a model of territorial concentration and jurido-political integrity. There are nations and ethnic groups that aspire to have states; there are those that straddle the boundaries of states; there are those that survive as diasporas. Communities of faith are generally dispersed, but may have a central reference point such as Rome, or sacred sites such as Jerusalem and Mecca. For many years, Moscow functioned in an analogous way as the heart of what Raymond Aron once called the 'ideocratic community' of world communism.

These general, analytical points are directly relevant to the interpretation of contemporary European reality, a space which has been divided along the fault lines of the Cold War, and those whose present shape remains unsettled, given that quite suddenly we seemingly live in a post Cold War world.

The dramatic and rapid transformation in the international climate associated with the Gorbachev-Reagan summits provided the crucial condition for us to begin to think that the Cold War was drawing to a close. In 1990, the official enmity between the West and East was declared dead. Maybe, as we look at the world and its instabilities in 1991, and watch the power struggles in the USSR with alarm and sadness, we should not rule out a new dusting-off of the old, familiar pictures of friends and enemies that filled our mental galleries but yesterday. Nevertheless, short of Soviet military adventurism aimed at recovering parts of the old socialist commonwealth, any future confrontation in Europe is not likely to be between blocs. So patterns of friendship and enmity on the continent are still likely to be different from those which came before. And consequently much less predictable. And therefore much more dangerous in certain respects.

At all events, as a result of detente and the revolutions of 1989, we have been given an important glimpse of what Europe might be when not divided by the Cold War. What has re-emerged from the grand divisions of yesteryear is Europe's complexity, one in which national, ethnic and religious diversity are striking in the extreme. The smell of unfinished business is once again in the air. In the east, and centre, states and nations do not enjoy a perfect fit. Nor do they in some parts of the West. How much of a problem this will be is impossible to predict. The Scottish political commentator Neil Ascherson has identified no less than forty-six potential flashpoints, not all composed of equally incendiary material by any means. At all events, it is in this context that we need to begin to think afresh about identities in Europe.

We do need to recognise the profound cultural consequences

that are being wrought by the end of the cold war, as these are bound to affect nations, states and collective identities. To take an obvious example, since 1989 one could not fail to be struck by the way in which 'Europe' in its larger sense has reappeared and no longer tendentiously designates the EC Twelve.

In fact, one of today's most significant debates, so far as any reshaping of Europe's structures of political identity is concerned, centres precisely upon the future of the European Community. What is tremendously striking is the way in which the debate had shifted here. The collapse of the GDR and its rapid *de facto* absorption into the Federal Republic at every level (and by extension into the EC itself), has clearly reshaped contemporary thinking about European economic and political unity. A united Germany, with a population of some eighty millions means that Europe's centre of gravity today will eventually shift to Berlin, not just economically but culturally and politically. In recent discussions with intellectuals from Paris, Madrid and Bologna I have already been told how marginal – nay peripheral – France, Spain and Italy will be. What then for Scotland or Ireland? (What suitable term should we find for Scotland? Outer Caledonian? And for Ireland? *outre*-Minch?) For their part, Poles and Hungarians recount that German-speakers are eagerly sought-after by enterprises, and that teachers of Russian are undergoing conversion courses to master the new *Handelssprache.* My paternal advice to my daughters is: '*Lernt Deutsch, und schnell!*' Of course, this may well be disregarded.

Small wonder, then, that some now ask whether the coming German hegemony over East-Central Europe will not strain the Community's coherence to breaking point.

Consequently, the political arguments between minimalist and maximalist views of the European community have major implications for our future sense of identity as 'Europeans'. The official minimalists, whose views were most lucidly and passionately expressed by Mrs Thatcher, favour market integration but do not like the implied political consequences, in particular the obvious diminution of national sovereignty. To put it in a nutshell, they remain nationalists. And, in Britain, it would seem, firm Atlanticists.

There is also a kind of unofficial EC-wide minimalism which takes the shape of an emergent White Continentalism (the first stirrings, perhaps, of a Euro-nationalism of the Haves?) firmly based on economic interests, but which also reinforces popular racism. As the internal market approaches completion, and internal borders lose their significance, the outer ramparts are going to be reinforced, for reasons of security (including counter-terrorism) and in order to control the growing pressure of immigration. With the inevitable future instabilities consequent upon large-scale population movements in Europe, from West to East and from the South to the North, this problem is not going to go away. One way of dealing with it, already apparent, is to demonise the (usually black or Asian) migrant. (But not only blacks or Asians: migrant East Europeans are already competing for unpopularity.) Even before the Gulf War, Islam had begun increasingly to take on an explicit political significance in European states in addition to its ethno-religious dimensions. One has but to think of the Rushdie affair in Britain, or in France,the exclusion from schools on Republican grounds, of girls wearing the chadoor. Moreover, of late, we have also borne witness to the revival of one of the oldest hatreds: the desecration of France's oldest Jewish cemetery at Carpentras signalled that in the West, too, there was no immunity to the widespread renaissance of anti-semitism across Europe.

The official national identities of existing states inside the EC do not look likely to vanish. One is also struck by tremendous resilience of the linguistic differences that these states underpin. One could stir the pot further by noting the existence of significant nations without states (such as the Scots, the Basques and the Catalans) in whose areas of territorial concentration autonomism and separatism of varying strengths remain on the agenda. I need hardly add that the conflict on this island seems unlikely to be resolved by the kind offer of a Euro-identity.

The maximalists' vision of a united 'Social Europe' is still alive and the drive towards an integrated political and economic community has taken on a new urgency as thought is given to changed relations with an expanded Germany. The integrationist vision clearly implies both the reorganisation of the North Atlantic Alliance and a rethinking of Community Europe's relations with the Soviet Union and the newly individualised states of the former Soviet bloc. But the likely outcome is far from clear, though the need to 'institutionalise' new diplomatic, security and economic arrangements is clearly recognised in the Chancellories of Europe.

In the course of the Gulf Crisis, however, it has become clear that military and diplomatic concertation are hardly easily achieved. The ultimate test of statehood is a monopoly of the means of violence within a bounded territory, and this does not seem imminent in Europe.

An analogous problem lies in the extent to which a European cultural space exists. This has been recognised by the Euro-bureaucracy whose main riposte has been to try and stimulate production of the moving image. If you go back to the origins of the idea of a 'European audiovisual space', you find that in substantial part it was stimulated by the dangers represented by US television imports. The worry is both economic and cultural. The cultural worry is that heavy viewing of American programming will erode the values and identity of EC Europe. America is seen as a cultural rival. The economic concern is about Europe's lack of competitiveness in the global market for symbolic goods.

Aside from the questionable imputation of an identity to EC Europe, the Brussels conception of audiovisual space is also underpinned by a rather mechanistic model of media effects that shows little awareness of the complexities of cultural consumption. What is the nature of this European culture that is to defend itself by such primitive means? So far, no-one seems to have successfully defined it.

The ideas about a European audiovisual space (which remains unrealised, despite some initiatives in supporting scripting and production) have had their analogues in other, competing products and projects. The New World Information and Communication Order first promoted by UNESCO in the mid-1970s worked on the basis of identical assumptions about dependency and resistance, except that then it was the Third World that sought to defend itself against the unequal flow of news and televised entertainment, rather than one element of the First World seeking to compete with another. A similar strategy was also at the root of the project of a 'Latin audiovisual space', launched in the early 1980s. In that case the symbolic and economic arguments were once again conjoined to propose 'Latin' audiovisual production to defend cultural identities threatened by a world market dominated by the 'Anglo-Saxons'.

Obviously, if the conception of a European audiovisual space is to be developed in accordance with change on the continent, it will have to embrace the larger, beyond-the-EC Europe. In other words, to recognise growing diversity as a starting point for the elaboration of its projects.

It is also now an increasingly open question how developments in the West will relate to the Soviet call for a 'common European home' or ' House of Europe' under whose roof some all-European security system might eventually emerge together with co-ordinated action over the environment, energy and communications. When this dream slogan was initially launched, Mr Gorbachev was speaking for what was still a bloc and was himself seen by Western states as the architect of positive change. The Soviet Union was being given the benefit of the doubt as a state in search of democratisation and structural economic reforms. Now as separatist problems mount inside the borders of the USSR, as the economy remains effectively unreformed, and repression is on the agenda, the place of the Soviet Union inside Europe looks more and more questionable.

In fact, the lines of future differentiation have already been sketched out in numerous quarters and are ready to be used. Back in 1984, the Czech novelist in exile, Milan Kundera, argued that Russia had no claim to be European, unlike the countries of Central Europe. It has been intriguing to see this idea echoed recently, with a direct foreign policy twist, by the military historian, Sir Michael Howard, and by the sociologist (and former EC Commissioner), Sir Ralph Dahrendorf.

Voices can now be heard in the USSR singing a reciprocal song: 'We are Euro-Asian. Why look to the West?' The gulf of mutual incomprehension and hostility is already opening up again in some quarters. Although not completely interred, then, one has the strong suspicion that the idea of a Common Home might be on its way to its final resting place. When first mooted, Western leaders leapt over one another to appropriate the phrase from the Soviet foreign policy makers. There is little sign of such interest now, a sure sign of its waning potency.

Whether common cause is to be made in Europe will depend particularly upon how far-reaching and how rapid the reform process in the Soviet Union can now be and on the kind of institutional anchorage that can be provided for the new expanded Germany. The grounds for optimism today seem less than in the *annus mirabilis* of 1989. The reassertion of the national dimension in the East and Centre of Europe also has a major bearing on the construction of a new European order. Aside from the undoubtedly positive aspects of national self-assertiveness after years of Stalinist and neo-Stalinist oppression, the negative dimensions have also been widely apparent, not least in intolerance towards ethnic and religious minorities.

It is sobering to reflect that a parallel fate to that of the Common European home appears to be overtaking the recent talk of a revived *Mitteleuropa* or Central Europe. This figured on the political and intellectual agenda in a number of countries on both sides of the Iron Curtain – in Austria and the Federal Republic and in Hungary and Czechoslovakia (and to some extent in Poland and Yugoslavia). As one might expect, there was never any one voice here, no unitary project or set of interests. Until late 1989, the idea of Central Europe was the pure province of intellectual fantasies: it aimed at the reconstitution of a plural civil society as a key central goal, and amongst the smaller states expressed a concern for defining a space between Russia and Germany. These issues are now in the realm of practical politics and need to be addressed with urgency. The outlook for building a civil society in conditions of economic scarcity and political uncertainty is not auspicious. At all events, for a moment, at least, the rediscovery of Mitteleuropa, like the proposal of a European Common Home, betokened a shifting of the normal mental frontiers to which we had become accustomed. With the collapse of the party-state regimes in much of East-Central Europe, new media markets have opened up. But here, the contradictions between the defence of renascent national cultures and identities and the invasive strategies of transnational corporations are bound to present tricky problems in the future.

Clearly, there is no denying the desirability of a new European settlement in which old enmities are interred and new friendships formed. However, we do need to be aware of the dangers of Eurocentrism. In the South, the shift of attention from the developing world to Eastern Europe has been keenly felt as a new process of exclusion, with potentially highly destabilising consequences.

Moreover, developments in Europe cannot be isolated from the wider task of reclassifying the so-called 'New World Order', but on the basis of different criteria from those that went before. For instance, the international relations expert William Wallace has suggested that the new First World will include the ex-socialist states of Eastern Europe, possibly many of the present Soviet republics, and a number of East Asian countries following the Japanese route to economic success. The Second World, he thinks, will be based in the Middle East, 'with claims to share an alternative ideology and culture', whereas the new Third World will be the truly wretched of the earth. This, of course, is a typical conjecture of the metropolitan elite, but quite plausible at that.

Within the existing First World, many tensions are apparent, not least between the United States, the EC and Japan. A sense of the present parameters of debate may be had by reading Paul Kennedy's *The Rise and Fall of the Great Powers* (1988). The 'declinists', such as Kennedy himself, believe that the United States has reached its zenith as a great power, both economically and militarily, whereas 'revivalists' believe that such talk is premature and that remedial action may still be taken. In addition to some redefined tripartite world order, in which the competition between Japan, the USA and a German-led Europe seems likely to be the driving force, North and South also seem set to do continuing work of macro-classification for some time. But these gross terms are just as open to the old objections as East and West were, and some new ones besides.

In the United States, there are clear signs of elite concern about how to deal with European political and economic competition at the global level. At the same time, there has been a growth in reciprocal negative stereotyping in the USA and Japan. The vision of a new tri-polar international capitalist world in which Japan, Europe and the United States fight it out may be exaggerated, but it clearly does present new possibilities for the displacement of the old Cold War enmities. In similar vein, occidental fears of Islam are also providing a new focus for redrawing the boundaries of friendship and enmity. The fact is that millions of Muslims live in 'Europe' and can hardly be excluded from being considered European.

A further macro-theme that I would like to introduce concerns the desecularisation of much contemporary political discourse. Putting it differently, religion understood as a cultural and political force is playing an increasingly prominent role in how we conceive of alignments and divisions, of friends and of enemies. A *locus classicus* of contemporary calls for the re-spiritualisation of the European continent came from Pope John Paul II speaking at Santiago de Compostela in November 1989. He proclaimed that 'European identity is incomprehensible without Christianity', which he characterised as at the root of the continent's civilisation and culture. This selective accentuation of the positive currently resonates more strongly in the vacuum left by the collapse of communist regimes in the old East, but is plainly not without many ambiguities for other Christian denominations than the Roman Catholic, for European adherents of other religions such as Islam and Judaism, and for non-believers in any religious creed at all.

One should not perhaps overstate the point, but there is also a sense in which the demise of Marxism-Leninism as an antithetical creed to capitalist democracy has been replaced by Islam, a point already suggested by nascent thinking of the Middle East as a new Second World of distinctive culture. The anthropologist Akbar Ahmed has observed that 'some of the free-floating hostility directed against communism over the last decades will move towards Islam'. The Gulf War has already demonstrated some of the potential dangers of a spiral of mutual hostility between what, in some quarters, are increasingly depicted as the Christian and Muslim worlds. Certainly, God has been heavily recruited to fighting units on both sides. I for one would prefer to hear nothing more about crusades and jihads. But I fear we shall. The point then is this: that in the near future we may well find that collective identities co-mingle cultural and religious differences in ways that we have not latterly been used to.

These wider movements will affect us all and will condition the elaboration of cultural politics and policies. They will inevitably affect the projects that television producers and filmmakers undertake in coming years. Sensitivity to complexity and tolerance of diversity might well be a good maxim to start off with. Where the journey will end remains an open question. Thank you.

DISCUSSION

James Hawthorne

My first duty, and it's a pleasant one, is to express collective thanks and appreciation for that paper from Philip Schlesinger. I think that he has opened up much that is new and much that is peculiarly relevant to our own tradition. He speaks of the process of inclusion, the process of exclusion, the creating of traditions, the activating of collective memories. I think these things touch us very closely indeed. Now we have a very widely disciplined audience, representing many fields, and it would be in the best interest of this symposium if we have a very broad debate with many taking part. I do hope, Philip, that Martin made it clear that you are now open to cross examination. In fact I also hope that you, the audience, can lay down some fresh points if you so wish because, when the shades of night fall fast later this afternoon, we have to consider the ultimate question, the Leninist question, at the end of the symposium, 'What is to be done?' If we can, through debate, take the practical steps towards some final conclusions, it will be an immense help and the day will have been well spent. So it is now open warfare either to ask Professor Schlesinger questions or to supplement what you have heard with any perspective of your own.

Tony Rowe: About Face Media Productions

I have come over from the mainland to set up an independent production company in Belfast, for all sorts of what I hope are very good reasons. It just struck me that throughout the professor's speech there seemed to be an emphasis that culture is used in a very negative sense. It is used as a weapon of discrimination rather than a means of cooperation. There seems to be a need for people to find a reason why they are different and therefore to exclude others. I say this because I was also was brought up in South Africa so I am aware of what apartheid and cultural division means. I would like to think that we can end this day with some sort of aspiration towards finding a way of creating a broader mosaic of cultures, where we all know what can be contributed to the greater whole and therefore making somehow a larger, more colourful, more alive society rather than fighting over one particular aspect, using our culture as a weapon over somebody else. I think what the professor said about sensitivity at the end is very important for media people because we are, I think, all of us, however much we try to fight it in ourselves, looking for a means of expressing *our* view and therefore might not be particularly sensitive to other views in order to make our story, in order to satisfy our pro-gramme buyer, in order to satisfy our editor. We have to, in all these things, somehow convey not our views but we have to act as an invisible medium of the culture to the people who need to be educated and informed. And maybe this is an anathema to broad-casters but I believe that tolerance has to tolerate the intolerant. As soon as you deny the intolerant an opportunity to be tolerated you immediately create conflict. It creates its own conflict but it is something that I think as communicators, which I think we are probably more than film makers, I believe our role should be to address that quite basic philosophy, that is that we should examine our role as purveyors of culture rather than using the culture for our own purposes. Thank you.

Bill Rolston: Lecturer in Sociology, University of Ulster at Jordanstown
Since we seem to have set the pace for the rest of the day, can I just say a word for intolerance, on behalf of intolerance? At least it may be taken as that! Cultures are arranged in hierarchies and whatever reason that might be, whether you see that as being due to economic factors, political factors, global/historical factors what-ever, I think that's a fact and I think it comes out clearly from most of what Philip Schlesinger was saying. For that reason it might be a function of researchers and media people to identify the intoler-ances, to parade intolerance, especially the intolerance of domi-nant cultures. Philip brought out the example of the new relation-ships between the north and the south of this globe. I am reminded of Billy Brandt's notion that we all live in one world and we have common interests and therefore we should not close ourselves off from each other. One response of southern economies was to say,

'Well look, sometimes we have to close ourselves off, to protect ourselves from you. Your economies are so strong that we'll never build our own unless we have some protective mechanisms.' I think that the in this notion of global tolerance, sometimes it's necessary to say, 'Look, even your claim of global tolerance is a form of intolerance. Let us work our own way too.'

James Hawthorne

There is surely a challenge laid down there. I hear the slipping of safety catches.

Elizabeth Johnston: M.A. Student, University of Ulster

Just an addition to the last comment that was made. I think it is obvious everywhere that tolerance has become a *tolerance of intolerance*. That is the case very much in regard to Islam for example, the whole Salman Rushdie affair. Also not just in the media but in general everyday life it has become a tolerance of the *intolerable*. It is too easy to go on about grandiose phrases like global tolerance without being aware what the dangers are that lie at the other end.

John Patterson: Student, University of Ulster at Coleraine

I just want to raise the point that maybe this sense of identity, this sense of imagined identity, whether it's an ideological one, one set by birth-place, space now occupied by religion, ideology etc, may actually tend to grow out of actual social conditions and that perhaps there is an identity that's underneath these others, that has got to do specifically with each community's social, cultural and economic needs. I wonder if Professor Schlesinger could comment on what he felt is the real identity behind it, if there is a real identity. If there is a sense of it beyond mouthing notions of a prehistoric past or whatever. An identity which comes out of the very specific economic and social conditions each community, or imagined community, are living through?

Philip Schlesinger

The point I was making about process, time and space as frameworks within which identities are constructed certainly suggests that I think that identities are social products, but they are not just things that you pluck out of the air. I think what was behind your question was whether identities constituted some sort of false consciousness, or something like that. Is that what you were getting at? Well they may do. You know, it's not a question you can resolve by definition, it's a question of obviously looking at given situations. They function as rallying points. They function as ways in which we may discharge emotion and sentiment and all sorts of complex feelings.

Going back to the earlier interventions that were made, I'm intrigued, but not surprised, that perhaps something that was a bit of an add-on was taken as the main point. 'Global tolerance' is not a phrase I use: you will find it no where in my text, indeed I challenge you to. I think that the point I was actually making, the real thrust of the argument, was that there has been a kind of delusion which we've been invited to share about Europe and its future and what this represents, and that once you actually start to look beyond the way this is presented to us in a lot of official talk, you actually find that there is this complexity, there are these inequalities, there are these imbalances, which we are going to have to confront if, you know, Europe is going to be anything.

I won't in any way deny the point that Bill Rolston has made - that cultures are unequal, or, putting it another way, some cultures are more equal than others and may have a preponderant place within a sort of global system of cultures. The question is obviously how you deal with that and there is no simple prescription. I think starting with the kinds of questions I am addressing, you go in for some sort of exploration of the differences and the sources of difference, rather than perhaps advocating that difference in itself implies that one or other group has predominance and that has to be fought. That's, if you like, an analytically separate point. I can see that it is an important political point, but I have addressed myself to what I think is the actual remit of the session. But, obviously, that is open to debate.

Catherine O'Neill: University of Stirling
As an Irish woman living in Scotland, I am well aware of the fact that most of the programmes we get in mainland Britain are about how divided the community is and I would be disappointed if this symposium so early lapsed into a discussion of how we might show

the divisions in Ireland and Northern Ireland. Obviously division is at the core of identity in Northern Ireland, but there is so much more to Northern Ireland than that. It is up to the people here, film makers, television script writers or whatever, to convince the people you work for, your editors and commissioning editors, that people in Britain are sick of hearing about the divisions in this community. Now I know it probably suits some people very well that people in Britain hear about how divided this community is, but we have much more to life in Northern Ireland than that. Even my supposedly enlightened friends in Scotland are always pressing me about what it is really like at home. All we are getting is the same old documentaries about division, about Catholics and Protestants, rather than people. You know, it can get a bit weary. Therefore, this is really a cry for help. If there are people here who do make programmes, could we have less hard-headed documentaries about division and maybe more programmes about real life. Thank you.

James Hawthorne
Well there is certainly a small cat been put amongst the pigeons there because there are programme makers here and I am sure they are bursting to address that issue. The problem of exporting Northern Ireland's image has always been a very big problem.

Paul Burgess: Community Relations Officer, Antrim
I was interested in the context of the idea of tolerance as an end in itself. I was recently involved in a research project at the University of Oxford, in the relationship between tolerance and moral development in school children. Several speakers referred to tolerance, and, desirable as it may well be, the indication was perhaps that was an end in itself. I think we would do well to remember, specifically in a Northern Ireland context, that it is quite possible to hold on to the concept of tolerance but that in itself may be a static not a positive concept. The Northern Ireland community is quite able to exercise a begrudging tolerance which in itself does little to further debate or to make progress towards solving divisiveness in this community.

Rod Stoneman: Commissioning Editor, Channel Four
I would like to go back to one of the points Martin McLoone made at the beginning about the notion of identity being in flux

and full of contradictions. I think that the angle of approach that's
been taken since, talks about identities at one level, without ac-
knowledging the strata of differentiation within any community or
within any individual. There are many Arabs that I have spoken to
who talk about being with Kuwait against Iraq, but with Iraq
against America. An Arab from the Maghreb, say, feels fully connected with the Arab family at large yet may feel different from
other parts of Arabia, in the Middle East – may feel political
difference between democratic traditions in say Tunisia and auto-
cratic structures in Iraq for example. Coming closer to home,
obviously national and cultural identities are at the centre of this
discussion but they should not to be, I think, discussed without
reference to class, gender and other forms of identity that come
into play. I mean it may be untactful to mention a film that was
made not very far from here that Channel. Four is only now
thinking about showing, called *Mother Ireland*[1] which was precisely
about the contradictions between the identities of feminism in
relation to the identity of republicanism in Ireland. I think that
the different notions of identity for any individual or for any group
– political, gender, class, nation, culture, – that those different
imaginary identities are in flux at any one time and I think that
that point that Martin McLoone made at the beginning is a dimension that mustn't be left out when we talk about the tectonic plates
moving around Europe.

Voice
   Can I ask you why the film hasn't been shown yet.?

Rod Stoneman
   Its a question that requires a long answer. Well I mean the most
simple answer is because of Douglas Hurd's ban, but I think it
would be disingenuous of me to pretend that Channel Four, in its
imaginary unity, was over-enthusiastic about showing the programme even before it was rendered problematic by Douglas
Hurd's ban. You could have guessed that.

Professor Robert Welch
   I just want to pick up on one of the last points made there
by that speaker, when he used that evocative phrase about the

tectonic plates moving around Europe in reference to Philip Schlesinger's talk. Indeed I think Professor Schlesinger put his finger on something I think very, very important in this sense, in his suggestion that identity is continuously moving. Fluid and mobile, it is subject to so many forces at any one time it is very difficult to still it or fix it. The danger is of course that those people, or those forces in ourselves which want to still it or fix it are the ones that we have to watch out for. I know we all have our own battalions of intolerance inside ourselves and it is very easy to project these out as well. One further point, not unrelated to what I have just said, and it's in relation to Philip's observation about mythologies. In the common acceptance now mythologies are a bad thing, and you can understand why people argue like this, attacking the 'myth' of the tribe of Europe, the myth of 1916, 1690 or whatever. These are dangerous forces and they can have galvanic powers; but myth, properly understood, tries to recognise that you have very powerful stories that people tell themselves at crucial moments of their sense of themselves and quite often when you look at mythology you are actually looking at a mobile series of interrelationships and stories and so forth. Even an apparently simple mythic element will have lots of contradictions hidden inside it and this is why I think that the stories that we tell ourselves, as long as these stories are not just simply driven by need or by self assertion, or by assertation over others, are actually trying to find new ways of thinking, of awareness and so forth. Then those myths or stories have in them that liberating element that James Hawthorne spoke about in relation to the imagination. It is possible, despite the fact of what Foucault and other people say, that you can have discourses which are not always striving for power. Sometimes when you read cultural commentators, sociologists and theorists you actually begin to think that all discourse, all political analysis, is a striving for power. But not necessarily. When you take into account the realm of imagination it is possible to conceive discourses there which are not totally preoccupied with assertion and power.

Tony Rowe

It seems to me that as a programme maker, and the rest of us here who are involved in programme making, I think, we have all reached a point where one is discussing the broadcaster merely accepting the kinds of programmes that are already being made. We have to somehow to address a means of conveying Irish culture and identity to a *different* culture and identity. One of the problems is that broadcasters, broadly speaking, are looking to satisfy their own audiences.

There is a complex communication problem here. On one hand, the programme maker has to identify his audience and therefore satisfy its preconceptions of the culture he wants to make a programme about. And yet he also wants to move that audience's perception of this culture on. That is why we have this problem where you don't see different kinds of programmes on the mainland. Mainland people want to see and expect a certain type of programme and a lot of programme makers, possibly on the island too, but certainly mainland programme makers, come over here because they want to make confrontational television. It will make their career – their professional name on the mainland.

People move from here to the mainland, they are Irish, they will therefore have to make programmes that will satisfy the by now traditional perception of the island. We have to somehow make the product from Ireland exciting enough to break through that barrier. The challenge is here as much as it is with mainland broadcasters. We have to change our perceptions of the sort of programmes that can come out of here – they certainly won't accept Irish dancing all the time, or those sorts of things, because they are considered parochial. There has to be a universality that we can perceive within the cultures here, within the identities of people here, in order to affect those on the mainland.

And they will grasp at it, I mean, in many ways, once the gap has been opened, they will grasp at it because they desperately want to see that there is a another side to life here. If programme makers believe that they are only in the game of pulling large audiences then the programmes will be confrontational. I suspect that is why the programme *Mother Ireland* wasn't accepted to some extent. There was a lot of controversy about it, but I'm not so sure that it actually satisfied the preconceptions of Northern Ireland.

Fionnuala Cook: National Council for Integrated Education
Just to make a point that Mr Rowe would offend our cultural identity less if he would stop calling this 'the island' and Britain, 'the mainland'.

Margo Harkin: Independent Producer
I was formerly with Derry Film and Video Workshop which made the programme *Mother Ireland*. You have just made the first point that I wanted to make. This vastly developing preoccupation in response to the speeches about us making product for Britain or the mainland is irrelevant. You have to be sensitive to the fact that there are people here who make programmes to explore their *own* notions of identity and make them for people in Ireland and that is very much at the nub of what this conversation will be about today.

John Patterson
This idea of consumption is perhaps one major problem. I have just completed research on Latin American theatre and there seems to be a revival of Latin American cultural exportation to Europe. What is in danger of happening with this culture at this end is just like third world-produced agricultural products which are exported to settle debt. The same thing is now happening to cultural products and this may be the result of a huge cultural machine, that includes the BBC and ITV around London, which needs to be fed. The danger is that we try to feed that machine instead of making programmes for the immediate community, very much small scale product. We will obviously keep on making the big programme, a big statement, and the machine itself that is eating this is stopping the rest of the country being fed in cultural terms.

Desmond Bell: Professor of Media Studies, University of Ulster at Coleraine
I think that the problem is not just consumption but also production. Because pressure is put on film makers in terms of budgets, whether these come from Channel Four or whether you are a BBC programme maker, to make a product which can be received/sold in the widest possible market place and some of the processes that Philip identified in the new Europe cultural markets are going to increase that particular pressure. Hence film production for regional audiences designed to challenge dominant representations, the sort of work of Margo Harkin and the Derry Film and Video group and also, I hope, part of the remit of

the Cultural Traditions Group, is up against a certain economic hard wall. I think we are all aware of that and I'm sure that the constraints of political economy will be one of the focuses for our discussions today. At this stage I want to flag the twin problems of the absence of adequate film funding in Ireland north and south and the difficulties that this lack of regional/national support creates for producers and directors who, in order to make films on Ireland have to negotiate with commissioning organisations whose interests are largely concerned with appealing to metropolitan audiences outside Ireland.

James Hawthorne

Time is all but spent. Coffee beans are popping in another part of the building – at least I hope they are.

If I may be allowed to invoke an administrative memory from my time with the BBC, a practical point about making films. It's perfectly moral and essentially practical to think about markets. Fundamentally you must tune your film to your audience, consider their perceptions and deliver your message in a form which can maximize their understanding of the actual subject you are tackling. We are conscious of visitors to our shores who don't always get our story right. I recall a French crew arriving in the newsroom at Broadcasting House in Belfast and asking to be taken to the Christian Quarter! The reply from behind a typewriter was: 'You'll have a job finding it in this town!' And then, in a spirit of cross-cultural *entente cordiale* he added 'Monsieur'.

Is there any final point you would like to add Philip?

If not, may I warmly and fervently thank you on behalf of this audience for setting us on our way on what I hope will be a valuable day.

NOTE

1. *Mother Ireland*, dir. Ann Crilly, Derry Film and Video Workshop for Channel Four, 1988. The film was subsequently shown by Channel Four as part of the *Banned* season, with the necessary changes to comply with the Home Office Guidelines issued by the Home Secretary, Douglas Hurd, in October 1988.

SESSION 2

Chair: Professor Desmond Bell

Media Studies, Coleraine

Broadcasting in Ireland – Meeting the Challenge

I have been asked to chair the second session which aims to address 'Broadcasting in Ireland: Meeting the Challenge'. Earlier Philip Schlesinger gave us a valuable global perspective on the shifting contours of cultural identity in Europe. Now we are going to address more specifically the regional and local interests associated with the media in Ireland. To help us address those issues we have a panel of distinguished broadcasters. From UTV we have Michael Beattie, commissioning editor for factual programmes, who most of you I'm sure know. We also have Bob Collins, Head of Television at RTE and lastly from Channel Four, we have Rod Stoneman the assistant commissioning editor in the independent film and video department of that company. What we propose to do in this session is to allow each of the three representatives of these broadcasting institutions the opportunity to map out their vision of broadcasting in the future and how they see their specific institution developing in the next few years in response to the not insubstantial economic, ideological and technological pressures now transforming broadcasting. Specifically we can ask how these changes in the organization of broadcasting will impact on programme making in Ireland. What will be the scope for innovative and critical programme and film making in Ireland? What role will broadcasting play in the future in exploring and interrogating cultural identity in Ireland?

Just to preface the discussion, I think it's worthwhile surveying quickly some of the dramatic technological and organizational changes occurring in broadcasting at the moment. In the South of Ireland the introduction of cable technologies and the high degree of cable penetration has led to a rapid expansion in channel availability. Cable developments are only now starting in the North, though it looks like it might expand very rapidly in the Belfast region in the next few years. On the other hand satellite dish installations have been more prevalent in the North. Either way in both regions we are witnessing audience fragmentation and the end of public service monopolies. The innovations in distribution technologies are not of course occurring in a political vacuum in Ireland. We have seen over the past few years a series of legislative changes, both north and south, most of which of course have been ideologically driven by a new enthusiasm for the market place and which have changed profoundly the face of broadcasting. We have seen the introduction of new patterns of media competition and new forms of media concentration. Some have sought to identify a terminal crisis in public service broadcasting. Others have identified opportunities for innovation. For one of the features of the new broadcasting legislation, particularly in the UK, though to a lesser extent in the Republic, has been the stipulation that broadcasters seek a proportion of their programmes from independent producers. Will this measure raise or lower the quality threshold of our television? Will it open up new points of access and allow new voices to be heard? What form will the new partnership between the channels and the independents take? What, more generally, are the prospects for the Irish film and television industry in a European television marketplace 'without frontiers' and increasingly without public service scruples? I would suggest that these issues might figure among the items of the agenda to be addressed in this session.

There are of course other complex political and cultural changes occurring today in this island of ours as we move towards 1992. Some argue that European integration offers exciting opportunities for broadcasters as it does for novel political realignments. Some argue that we are witnessing the end in the Republic of Ireland of the long night of authoritarian nationalism and civil war politics. In the north they perceive also a new sense of tolerance and questioning of traditional loyalties and of the sectarian divide. Others are perhaps less optimistic and argue that, given the unresolved nature of the national question in Ireland and our continued economic dependency, cultural development continues to be impaired by our post-colonial status, stuck in a certain trough of despondency. Broadcasters are also responding to these currents and we must continue to hope that television will manage to provide a central forum for cultural and political debate in Irish society as it has in the past. Despite the pressures towards commercialization and homogenisation in TV output that we can identify today hopefully we can retain in the discussions that follow optimism with regard to the cultural role of television in our society – an optimism of the will, perhaps always necessarily tempered by a pessimism of the intellect.

I call firstly Michael Beattie, from UTV, to give his presentation.

MICHAEL BEATTIE

Commissioning Editor, Ulster Television

Quite a few years back when I worked as a reporter, I was in a studio on one occasion with a rather large and prominent cleric and politician and it was in the days when he was particularly savage on most people who interviewed him. To kill a few minutes before the studio was ready to record I said to him, because we had been discussing this, 'Dr Paisley has anyone actually ever got the better of you in an interview?' He laughed and he said, 'Yes, the first couple of interviews I ever did, because I answered the questions I was asked'. I think there's a lesson there for all of us and I can assure you that not being a politician I always try and answer the questions that I am asked. But I have to say that there are certain difficulties about going too far into how Ulster Television is meeting the challenge which is the title of this session. I am afraid that to disappoint Martin, I am going to, of necessity, have to bring in the filthy lucre.

What I would like to do is to be fairly specific and to suggest a concise and perhaps precise definition of what the challenge is, particularly to regional broadcasters, and the challenge comes in the main as has been outlined from two of the issues listed under the wider changing context in this symposium literature 'The transnational nature of broadcasting technologies and deregulation of broadcasting'. What they have together succeeded in doing, and this is more of a personal view or statement based on my experience of the industry, what they have succeeded in doing, is to present the most basic challenge of all, survival. For 18 months or more the broadcasting press has been carrying stories of redundancies, now running into thousands throughout Great Britain, both in independent television and the BBC. In fact the most recent report I saw was about 200 job cuts in BBC Wales. Now within the ITV system some of this, at least, can be put down to preparation for the new round of contract auctioning. To use a hackneyed phrase companies becoming 'leaner and fitter' for the increasingly competitive and cost-conscious broadcasting environment ahead. Every ITV company is fighting for its survival. You will probably all be aware that Ulster Television already has one rival consortium out in the open and others may well surface in the weeks ahead,[1] and it will be weeks ahead because applications for the contracts have to be submitted in April. So I am afraid that just in case that there are any moles here, what I am not able to do is to outline any five year plan or ten year plan that Ulster Television may have. I'm afraid that that's going to have to remain under wraps until April when our application, and who knows how many others, are safely consigned to the ITC.

When many broadcasters are willingly, deliberately, becoming leaner and fitter, independent television is also feeling the pinch or maybe a heavy nip as the recession continues to have a severe effect on advertising revenue and just as an aside, while that hit ITV generally from before the start of last year, it didn't really come home to Ulster television until after the summer. And it is a severe decline. It seems that this recession is unlikely to be a short term one and as income declines, ultimately, that means less money for making programmes.

But one of the interesting points becoming apparent from these continuing lists of redundancies is that they aren't having a significant impact in the areas of news and current affairs. Drama, yes, light entertainment, documentaries, technical staff of all kinds, but it's clear that the broadcasters aren't so keen to tamper with the oft maligned news and current affairs departments. So why is that? Well I think it's because there's a view abroad that local news and current affairs will be one of the main areas, and possibly the main area, to attract a local audience not too far down the road when that audience will have a great many more channels to choose from. As choice grows, broadcasters become increasingly concerned about ratings and perhaps it may be the case that to keep an audience in order to survive, a regional broadcaster will decide to transmit more acquired quiz shows, sit-coms (and that's not local sit-coms because they're too expensive), repeats, froth of every kind, creating more uniformity and less regional distinctiveness. While I can't recommend its literary style, I found this book very interesting and it actually glances over some of the points raised by Professor Schlesinger '*Mega Trends 2000 – the next ten years – major changes in your life and work*' (John Naisbitt/Patricia Aburdene, Pan 1990).

'Seventy five per cent of all imported tv comes from the United States. The potential of global television and the massive export of American television shows leads to least common denominator programming and the homogenisation of culture. Will it threaten the differences that make individual countries interesting, will it facilitate the tendency for powerful countries like the United States to impose their values on third world and other countries, or will it bring a backlash? Unlike cheese burgers and jeans, the globalisation of television is explosive and controversial because it conveys deeper values the way literature does. Entertainment through the medium of language and images crosses over the lines of superfluous exchange and enters the domain of values. It goes right to the ethos of a culture, addressing the fundamental spirit that informs its belief and practices'. You may not like the style but you know the point.

So let's for a moment speculate that a regional broadcaster concentrates his *local* production effort on news and current affairs and let's look at that area for a moment in relation to culture and identity. And coincidentally, while I didn't attend the Cultural Traditions Group conference 'Variety of Irishness', the report of the seminar on communications clearly seems to suggest that the greatest degree of concern was voiced about the areas of news and current affairs.[2] Now obviously any wide-ranging news and current affairs department gives expression to a variety of people, from a variety of backgrounds, reaffirming and so giving definition to their culture and also, despite the confines of news and current affairs, the people making those programmes are not a uniform breed. But it would seem that while those kinds of programmes may gain the local audience that this speculative regional broadcaster wants, it leaves a lot less opportunity for films and programmes which are specifically about the culture of the island and the issues of identity, less room (to pinch an expression from Michael Longley who used it at a meeting I was at one night, and I thought it was tremendous) to show people 'it wasn't always like this', and less time for the deeper exploratory, radical programmes many people would like us to see and some people would suggest there isn't enough time for even now.

But all that is only speculation. One can also speculate that whoever a new ITV contractor may be in 1993 that a sufficiently high audience of local people will desire those programmes which go further in exploring the issues to justify making those programmes. Perhaps the advertising revenue and finance from whatever source will make it possible to increase output in quantity or quality. There are those who suggest the audience *will* be sufficiently discerning to choose locally-made programmes instead of turning on to their sports channel, their movie channel, their video channel, what ever it may be. It's all speculation and you can speculate either way. For a commercial broadcaster very little can be certain at the moment.

But news and current affairs do form the core of any regional broadcaster's output. Beyond that the Independent Television Commission require certain other areas to be attended to as part of the new contract for 1993. The quality threshold, although sometimes I think it's more of a quantity threshold, lists a variety of areas which must be covered, but how well will they be covered?

It is obviously Ulster Television's desire, and presumably the desire of any regional broadcaster, to cover the broadest possible range of programming. The financial future will dictate how far we, or any one else, can go in those aspirations. I would like to agree with the comment, an appeal, made by Mary Holland at the Varieties of Britishness conference when she said 'I would like to ask for the air waves, for the media, to be open to everybody'.[3] I think that that's probably what all of us desire and aspire to. Now however constrained we may be in the future there has to be a place for the widest possible expression of views, for programmes which may not be justifiable purely in terms of audience. But I'm not just talking about programmes that might be buried at half past midnight. There has to be an area, perhaps not in peak programming time but certainly in easily accessible programming time, where those programmes which don't demand a big audience should have a place. I was glad of a comment, if I can quote from the Varieties of Irishness report. 'We could have talked until the cows came home about individual tastes in news and current affairs, about indigenous documentaries and we would have expressed strong wishes about how the broadcasting institutions might promote cultural diversity, but we did realise there is nothing we can do really about them. Media institutions will run their own affairs and the only course open to us is one of continual dialogue and persuasion'. Well I'm glad at least we seem to be open to dialogue and persuasion and in conclusion I will just quote once again from this report. 'We know that research shows media is not as brain-washing as we might think, that in the pre-school age groups, youngsters' ideas are formed and there is no strong evidence that fundamental beliefs and attitudes are later influenced by the media'. I am not so sure. In 1983 the Tuareg, the largest nomadic tribe in the Sahara, delayed for 10 days their traditional annual migration across the desert – in order to catch the last episode of *Dallas*. Thank you.

NOTES

1 UTV was challenged for the Northern Ireland franchise by two consortia – TVNI and Lagan Television. Although outbid by its competitors, UTV successfully saw off the challenge and was awarded the franchise on the 'quality threshold' clause.

2 Maurna Crozier (ed.), *Cultural Traditions in Northern Ireland : Varieties of Irishness*, Belfast, Inst. of Irish Studies, 1989.

3 Maurna Crozier (ed.), *Cultural Traditions in Northern Ireland : Varieties of Britishness*, Belfast, Inst. of Irish Studies, 1990.

BOB COLLINS

Director of Television Programmes, RTE

Philip Schlesinger said that if you can say the word intellectual and keep a straight face you must be on the continent. Perhaps a more recognisable version of it might be that if you can say the word anti-intellectual and know that you are targeting the dominant forces in the establishment you must be much closer to home.

I have to begin by apologising for the fact that I don't have an erudite and carefully prepared and skilfully crafted piece of script for you and you will have to make do with some possibly scattered observations. I know also that we are operating under a time scale or time limitation and at the outset let me apologise for the fact that I am going to have to leave here at lunch time because I have to be back in Dublin tonight. Given the nature of communication, in the other sense, in this island it's very difficult to do that without getting out of here very quickly.

I think the most important thing I want to say is that in relation to where we stand and how we face the future, in RTE specifically, but I think in the broadcasting community on this island in general, we are having great difficulty in coping with the anti-intellectualism which is dominant around us and that the notion of a role for broadcasting is no longer a given in public life in the way that it was. I believe that the perception of the role of broadcasting is at the centre of any debate about the future and I'm afraid that in the last 10 years, perhaps even in the last 5 or 6 years, there has been a dramatic shift within Europe as a whole, within what used to be Western Europe, but certainly increasingly now our friends in Eastern Europe are going to find the cold wind reaching them. In Britain also, courtesy not least of her former excellence Mrs Thatcher and in the fashion that has characterised us for a very long time, if Britain moves can Ireland be far behind? Not a lot when it comes to the development of social and cultural policy. There is now a pervasive sense of commercial value in the approach to broadcasting and broadcasting policy. That is not to say that broadcasting organisations which derive their income in whole or in part from the transmission of commercials are necessarily, or at all, embracing commercial value. We take half of our revenue from broadcasting advertisements and the other half from licence fee: the ITV system in Britain is in the mainstream of the public service approach. But the commercial values which characterise American television and which characterise satellite programming with which we are now becoming increasingly familiar, are pervasive, I think, in public policy in relation to broadcasting. For me that is a view which I find very difficult to accommodate. Broadcasting, communications, television, radio (and we shouldn't forget radio in these discussions), are key elements in society and there is a significant social role for broadcasting and the purpose of a broadcasting service, certainly in a community like this but in any community I would argue, is one which addresses the issues which are relevant to the community which it serves. It exists in the pubic interest not in its own interest. It doesn't exist in the interest of share holders nor in the interest of government nor in the interest of the state nor in the interest of those who ultimately determine the amount of money which it gets, and who can pay the piper and who would like also to call the tune.

Its purpose should be to explore the issues which are relevant to the lives of people, to address the concerns which people have, to open windows on the world, to expose isolationism and chauvinism, to ask questions which underlie the way life is lived and particularly to give people an opportunity to talk to themselves, to recognise themselves and to have a sense of their own value, purpose and identity which is not part of some large amorphous whole : of some mass audience. This is, I regret to say, an increasingly unfashionable view and is regularly abused as being naive and out-moded, an attitude which I continue to try to challenge. The usefulness in events such as this, meetings such as this, is to expose the contemporary view to challenge because it is all too easy to absorb, to take on board, what appears to be the dominant ethos of the moment. The market is not an adequate measure of what broadcasting should be about and I think that there is a particular concern in relation to programming for children. Increasingly, European broadcasters, public service broadcasters, are withdrawing from the area of children's programming. Less and less of programme budgets are devoted to children's programmes. Less and less locally made children's programmes are available. More and more use is being made of internationally-produced material whose principal purpose is to allow the sell-through of other products rather than to provide a service for the children at whom they are broadcasting. If this were to continue children will have a greater sense of American and Australian communities or pseudo-communities than they would of the communities from which they themselves come. I think, then, that there is a dangerous and sinister and insidious erosion of the notion of television as having a significant role to play in the lives of children which has to be resisted.

The difficulties about these fine sounding and high minded notions is that, notwithstanding Martin's desire that we not sully our brains, let alone our hands with filthy lucre, they are quintessentially inseparable from and linked to the funding of broadcasting and of audiovisual production and expression in the broadest sense. It is inadequate to say that this is simply a commodity, this is simply a product which has no greater attribute than any other product, no greater responsibility than one would prudently expect of any other product on the market place. I am afraid that the challenge facing us in Europe as a whole, certainly in Ireland, is the challenge, not just of survival as Michael said, and that is very much true, but the challenge of persuading the audience that broadcasting is important in their lives, not because broadcasters are important, because they are not, but because the role that broadcasting and communication have in community life is significant. Given the role and interdependence and inter-relationship between communications and the community, if you change broadcasting structures and control you change the community. The consequences of that are frequently invisible until after the event when it is too late. Professional broadcasters have been too slow in identifying the significance of analysis and evaluation and examination of the communications process for their audiences, not to preach to them, nor to speak down to them [and to fill voids in their lives] but to begin the process of evaluating the significance of what we are about. Until we win the support of our audiences we are unlikely to be able to win the support of our governments. I think that one of the real challenges that faces us is in maintaining heart in the face of vigorous opposition, in maintaining an open dialogue with our audiences in terms of what it is that broadcasting is there to do and in resisting in a vigorous way the blandification, the Americanisation, the 'decontentisation' of what we transmit. I think that all of these are more than usually relevant on this island where the existence of intercommunal misunderstanding and conflict and separation are so much evident around us, where also there are a range of cultures sitting side by side, where there is a minority language seeking an opportunity of expression in a way which isn't condescended to or in a way which doesn't have to be apologetic: the reality of our lives is going to be much more difficult in the future as far as each of those is concerned.

I think also we have to address, and from our perspective in RTE we have to address, the extent to which we have discharged the responsibility which is imposed on us by our Broadcasting Act, which is to be responsive to the interests and concerns of the whole community, be mindful of the need for understanding and peace within the whole island of Ireland and ensure that the programmes reflect the varied elements which make up the culture of the people of the whole island of Ireland and so on. I think that in relation to the extent to which we do reflect the values and cultures of the people of this part of the island of Ireland we probably have not been as successful as we should have been and we may not have been even as diligent or as attentive as we should have been. I think that there is not only a partition in the sense of a physical boundary on the island but there is a partition in the sense of mentalities on the island. This is not a political statement it is simply a reflection of the way people tend to live and breathe and think. The British Midlands crash tragedy two years ago I think captured it for me. If that had been an aircraft leaving Heathrow directed at Dublin airport and had crashed in the same circumstances, with the same numbers of people – with the same identical people on board – I think the response that we would have made as broadcasters, and the response which the community, the media community would have made would have been quite different from that which actually happened. Of course it was covered, of course there was a sense of loss, a sense of grief, a sense of grieving with people who were bereaved, of course there was a sense of the awfulness of the tragedy, but there wasn't the same sense of engagement with it as if it had been, as I say an aircraft which was coming to land in Dublin. That's in once sense, a remote point, but it does reflect the fact there are many aspects of life in Northern Ireland which we do not reflect. The largest of our non-Dublin, to call them that, offices or bureaux is in Belfast and we have been making a very positive attempt in recent years to move away simply from coverage of conflict and to attempt to reflect the lives of ordinary people, and the ordinary lives of people. We have in the same few years been attempting to increase the levels of contact between ourselves and BBC Northern Ireland and with UTV in areas which are unrelated to conflict, and I am glad to say that there has been a very substantial growth in the area of co-production between us, with both BBC and UTV in a way which I think helps us to present some sense of each others identity to our respective audiences. In response to Martin's obliquely-posed question at the very beginning of today's symposium, I don't think we have satisfactorily reflected the interests and concerns and cultures and traditions of the unionist community in Northern Ireland and that is an area to which we have to give substantial attention. We have, of course, been accused of giving vastly too much attention to the unionist tradition, at various stages, in our news and current affairs programming, but I don't believe, taking any objective evaluation, that that is a valid summation of what we have been doing.

To conclude, because I think I am in danger of overshooting my time, I think the challenge that we face is one of maintaining the meaning of broadcasting as we have traditionally known it, not being unwilling to change, not being unwilling to shift, to share power, not being unwilling to accept a greater presence of independently-produced material, not being afraid of structural, control and regulation changes, but holding on to the purpose and meaning of broadcasting. We must maintain the importance of broadcasting in the community, the importance of communications and the importance of the process in which we are engaged. We have also to justify, first of all to justify and then actively to seek, the support of our audiences in imposing on governments and powers-that-be, the kind of broadcasting arrangements which will enable the kinds of programmes to continue to be made which people want. The range of issues that Philip Schlesinger identified in his address this morning, the resonances in Ireland of what is happening in central and eastern Europe are multiple, yet the likelihood is that if things go as they are we will not be in a position to explore those issues. We would not be in a position to ask those questions, we would not be in a position to make the programmes that will give our audiences a sense of themselves, but more importantly a sense of their place in the wider world. That is, I think, our critical task, as well as taking hard decisions in the context of the resources we have, of resisting the temptation to schedule purely for competitive purposes, in resisting the temptation to marginalise and perpheralise programmes which will not attract mass audiences. Because if one thing more than anything else characterises what public service broadcasting is about it is the recognition that the audience is not an undifferentiated whole, but a series of interlocking minorities with a series of interlocking interests, needs, concerns, all of which have to be reflected in broadcast output. That is what will, at the end of the day, represent the real distinction between broadcasters with a sense of public service and those which have a purely commercial approach, which operate only by commercial values. The challenge for us is to continue to see our audience not as a large mass in the distance but as a series of small units that characterise the sense of community which is our touchstone. Thankyou.

ROD STONEMAN

Commissioning Editor, Channel Four

I would just like to begin by saying 'paper' isn't quite the right term for what I am going to deliver given that I was only invited to speak a short time ago, so therefore these comments are inevitably going to be improvised and rather sketchy. Indeed if I had known I was going to be filling in for the BBC, I would have worn a tie!

If I may begin in a rather personal and anecdotal vein. I experienced an extraordinary deja vu coming along to this conference this morning because last year, by fortuitous connection, I went to see some independent film makers in South Africa and I arrived there on a Sunday in November and found myself being taken, in a rather confused and jet-lagged state, to a hall not unlike this and sitting in on a conference not unlike this. It was called *Broadcasting in a Divided Community*, and had been set up as part of a process of community dialogue that Van Zyl Slabbert's Institute for Democratic Alternatives and the Campaign for Open Media has initiated; it's not unlike the Cultural Traditions Group here and brought together the same sort of mix of academics, independent producers, broadcasters as this conference. It was certainly an astonishing experience to see the two South African CP's, the virtually racist Conservative Party and the recently legal Communist Party, on the same platform and actually both agreeing that the main task at hand was to break apart and open up the monolithic South African Broadcasting Corporation (the institutional broadcaster that runs the two channels in South Africa) to a more diverse range of political views.

Obviously it's not absolutely analogous but there were certain points of resonance for sure. Another example which struck me – people may think that C4, UTV, RTE represent 'fortress television' and are difficult to communicate with or to penetrate, but the actual physical building of the South African Broadcasting Corporation looks very much like the Andersontown police station, with vast towers, barbed wire and gun emplacements all around it, so it was an immediate visual recognition for me – the State under siege.

Another aspect that I immediately recognised, when listening and discussing broadcasting possibilities with small scale independents in Cape Town and Johannesburg was not just the usual pressure and hunger for proper finance to make their own programmes but in a certain kind of heightened frustration and fiercer anger that immediately rang the bell for me – I thought I was right back in Belfast or Derry! I think that the connection is that of two societies which have become media spectacles because of the violent and political conflict that fissures them. Presumably if you live in, say, Brittany or Bologna there are not too many film making opportunities there either. But independents living and working in Belfast or Johannesburg are even more frustrated because their social contexts are represented on the television screens of the world quite a lot of the time. For small independents it is particularly frustrating as, if they do have any role, it's probably being hired to produce images which are then sent back to be processed and reconstructed in another place a long way away. The feeling of lacking economic and creative and editorial control is exacerbated in that process.

I hope that in the last five or six years with the effect of C4, UTV, RTE and BBC beginning to open towards independents in different ways and at different rates, this situation is changing somewhat. It will be interesting to see from the discussion today how that process is assessed from the independents' point of view because it does seem that there is still a long way to go.

One reason for my starting point, discussing the work of small independents to the changing coverage of Northern Ireland, but also to most communities and cultures in conflict, is based on my sense that independent work is arguably, if not provably, different from other prevalent representations. I would contend that if, like Martin McLoone, you sat viewing tapes at the Celtic Film Festival, in a kind of blindfold test without seeing the credits at the end of the programmes, you could tell from the programmes themselves which were made by independents and which were made by HTV, BBC Scotland, Grampian. In other words (present company excepted) the bigger, larger scale broadcasters.

I would contend that, in the main, work produced by independents has a sharper focus, is often more imaginative and original aesthetically and sometimes has a greater sense of polemic or point of view. This is to do with the process of production located outside large scale institutions, allowing for sometimes a better sense of the texture of everyday life and particularly the contradictions that cut through everyday life in a place like this. Is it just an empty assertion to suggest that, by and large, independently made programmes manifest these advantages, which are visible from a careful viewing of the programmes themselves? I think they arise from two factors: the actual position of small-scale independent producers in the world they seek to represent and their specific mode of production.

Smaller units, groups and individuals live and work as an integral part of their communities. Film production teams are closer to the activities and views and have a significant role in the cultural life of their communities. This inevitably affects the way that people will talk to and work with the group when collaborating on a production. These relations are less easily attainable by those working in larger broadcasting institutions which are precisely more formidable and less familiar to the community.

The mode of production also differs in scale, structure and often in pace; allowing a more reflective and responsive form of work. In some cases programmes are built collaboratively over a long period of time – showing and discussing the individual elements to people involved.

To come back to the debate about the imaginary unities of cultural identity in this conference, independent productions are able to often offer a finer sense of the complexity and contradictory nature of the factors which constitute identities. Independents are, in my view, especially well positioned to explore these factors as they view them from a more oblique angle than institutional broadcasters. A more uncomfortable and dialectical point of view from which one can open up the fissures and ambiguities that traverse the identities of this particular territory.

However, in this situation, in order to represent the basic protagonists in a very long-term and violent wasteful conflict, those protagonists must be identified and their views presented, which isn't exactly helped by the British government's Broadcasting ban, and the Irish government's Section of 31[1] which enmesh broadcasters in myriad legal and editorial problems and impede any attempt to make clear and direct presentation of the views of some of the relevant protagonists in the conflict.

Beyond that initial exposition it is necessary to tease out the flux, the contradictions, the complexities about, for example being precisely a women and being a republican (*Mother Ireland*)[2], or seeking to explore progressive traditions within the protestant community (*Redeeming History*)[3], or being in a society which most of the dividing lines are expressed in religious forms which you reject (*Moving Myths*)[4], or being a socialist in southern Ireland (*Ireland-Trouble the Calm*)[5] or (I can't summarise it in a sentence) some of the impossible sexual and political contradictions experienced by young people growing up in Derry depicted in a recent imaginative fiction film (*Hush-a-Bye-Baby*)[6]. This example reminds me that we should not just be talking about documentary and current affairs here – fiction and other hybrid forms of the audiovisual are equally adept at being able to articulate the levels and complexities, shifts and movements between the different layers of imaginary unities and identities which exist socially. In some cases the fault lines of identity lead to forms of political and violent conflict. Any individual's subjectivity is moving through (and is moved through) these dynamic patterns of identity. The major categories of gender, race, class and culture are constructions which we all inhabit in different combinations.

Indeed individuality and difference are constituted by the shifts within combinations of these fields of force. We are aware, here for instance, of the movement between the categories 'Nationalist' and 'Republican' when whole communities shift ambiguously between the two depending on the general context of the conflict and even specific recent incidents. A particularly dramatic atrocity (Bloody Sunday, Enniskillen) perceptibly informs the attitudes and feelings of Turf Lodge and Craigavon and perhaps also Waterside and Short Strand.

It may well be a contentious statement to assert that independent film makers from their position in the world and the process of film making that they are engaged in, are more able to articulate these areas of complexity. This assertion also leads me to privilege indigenous independent producers in any given situation. The use of such producers cannot be rigidly exclusive because occasionally there are valuable and interesting insights to be made by film makers from outside. But generally it seems to me that the more interesting and more authentic voices comes from inside. For example, after media preoccupation with the process of Europe moving into the new configuration, questions of north/

south relations may return to the front of the longer term agenda. Broadcasters will have to learn to listen to the voices of the South and not just send more crews of parachute journalists out to Africa, Asia or Latin America but actually find ways of looking at the indigenous film and video making of producers from those continents directly.

As I say, this discourse is a bit rambling because it is produced at short notice. But to finish the question of identity, I would futuristically dream of a utopia whereby differences that I have been talking about – cultural, national, political, gender, class, and a myriad of others -are enunciated with greater vividness and greater separation, with greater specificity, but are not arranged hierarchically. We are all characterised differently but no one would be better or worse to be male or catholic, homosexual or working class. As someone said in the debate after Philip Schlesinger's paper this morning, the problem with differences is they are normally arranged in a highly hierarchical order. This is indeed something of a formal problem because I do not even know how to write a non-hierarchical list because one word has to be either above or to the left hand side of another! We think in categories and inevitably those categories are bound into (and bind us into) hierarchies. But while it's very difficult to imagine how we can achieve that imagined utopia of freely formed difference one can certainly move in its direction, starting with programmes which address specific audiences in their diversity and sharpen and express the separation of cultural identities a little better than is done at present.

If the above is the theory, the actual practice which might help realise it would also involve forming a new organisational unity in a lobby of independent producers from Ireland rather like the well organised Scottish independents and the original alliance of independents which led to Channel Four coming into being in the first place and has since moved on to push some of the larger monolithic, pre-existing broadcasters to ingest a space for independents within their programming. This work has to be achieved by a group of independents constituting themselves, whatever their other differences, around the unity of a shared desire for a range and diversity of programmes to reach the screen. I haven't heard that kind of voice from Ireland north, south or together. I think that if that lobby was constituted, it would be able to focus very strongly on the public service criteria which, despite a decade of Thatcher, all broadcasters still maintain (even our current and future colleagues on Channel Three). They must push for the range of programmes they want to make and for serious programmes, which address different audiences and have a bit of imagination and polemic, to be transmitted before 12 o'clock at night.

So when some future version of a lobby of independents from Ireland talks to broadcasters, instead of just arguing about specific projects it may also choose to talk about why a whole strand doesn't work for this reason or was unbalanced for that reason or how this opinion was left out. That's a form of address which can't be so easily avoided by broadcasters on financial grounds. However, while we mention finances it is true that it's tougher now, for the whole ITV system is under pressure as advertising revenue has dropped substantially in the last year. It has to be said that truth is not the only casualty of the Gulf War, as recently every available budget within Channel 4 has been clawed back for contingency to pay for coverage of the land campaign in Iraq – should that happen.

It is rather disingenuous for me to be proposing a lobby on broadcasters but faced with increasing financial pressures, all broadcasters are more constrained in their choices. But the key thing is really about the range of strategies that are worked out for the finances and resources that one has; this is true no matter what pressure there is on them, how diminished the pot is.

I will wind up just by saying that I think it's a question of constituting new forms of cultural identity, within groups of independent producers, carrying it through to put pressure on the particularly relevant points in broadcasting organisations and en route conferences like this seem to be exemplary in formulating such an engagement. It is also crucial to make sure that the broadcasters are not merely being pushed by certain politicians into being market led. I am afraid that the new Broadcasting Act in Britain *can* be interpreted as a strategy which avoids directly forcing the broadcasters to change the political or cultural shape and texture of their programming but which releases market forces which in the longer term will achieve the same ends.

I think that broadcasting institutions, unlike most political parties these days, should be clear that they have the responsibility of leadership rather than just following market research. Taking decisions on the basis of what you think could or should be done rather than what the 'market' allegedly thinks it wants, can be surprising sometimes. Just one example from a fortnight ago because it's also near at hand: we showed a programme called *Travelling People*[7] which is a fairly polemical critique of the way that the Northern Irish and the Southern Irish administrations relate to travellers and it would appear from the BARB figures that 1.3 million people watched it at 11 o'clock at night, which to be honest is probably also helped by the 3 million people watching *The Manageress* immediately beforehand which is a useful hand-over into the programme. But that does not entirely explain it because most factual programmes on Channel Four at peak time, let alone at 11 o'clock at night, let alone about travellers in Ireland would not normally achieve that audience.

I guess you will have spotted that I am trying to have my cake and eat it, as I would prefer not to contest commissioning and scheduling decisions on grounds of audience and market, but if one has to, perhaps one needn't be too afraid because some of the independent programmes that fulfil the criteria I have been talking about, do connect with a large scale audience in a pleasurable way.

NOTES

1 Section 31 of the Broadcasting (Amendment) Act 1976 (Ireland) prohibits interviews with members of named organisations, including Sinn Fein, IRA, UVF and UDA. The legitmacy of this has been challenged in the European Court by the NUJ with the support of the Director General of RTE. The result of this challenge is pending at time of going to press.
2 *Mother Ireland*, Anne Crilly, Derry Film and Video Workshop.
3 *Redeeming History: Protestant Nationalism in Ireland*, Desmond Bell, Glass Machine Productions.
4 *Moving Myths*, Cathal McLaughlin, Belfast Film Workshop.
5 *Ireland-Trouble the Calm* Dave Fox, Faction Films.
6 *Hush-a-bye Baby* Margo Harkin, Derry Film and Video Workshop.
7 *Travelling People*, Michael Quinn, Northern Visions.

DISCUSSION

Martin McLoone

In preparation for this symposium, I did a little bit of field research, modest I might add, since I conducted it within my own extended family. But I asked a simple question. 'If you didn't have to pay the licence fee, would you mind that BBC1 and BBC2 had advertisements?' The answer was a clear, one hundred per cent 'No, we wouldn't mind!' Now obviously that was the response of a small group of people but I have no doubt that it reflects the opinion in the UK as a whole in relation to BBC and probably in the South as well, in relation to RTE.

Now obviously, it is a simplistic question, but I suspect it confirms my view that there is no great public support for public service broadcasting. How, then, does one convince the general population that paying the licence fee is in their interests? In other words how do you advertise the notion of public service broadcasting to a general population which doesn't seem to understand it, or to give it any great level of support?

Bob Collins

I think that if there were an answer to that question it would have solved a lot of problems a long time ago. Clearly if you ask people if they would prefer not to pay the licence fee I would be surprised if they said 'Oh I'm happier with things the way they are'. Would you prefer not to have to pay for a pint? Yes! Ideally if you could pay the licence fee in the same way that you pay for a whole lot of other things ie spread over twelve months or twenty six fortnights or fifty two weeks, through bankers orders or whatever, it would be preferable than paying all of it in one payment. In addition, a disproportionate number of people renew their licences near to Christmas because that's when they bought the television in the first instance; that is a bad time of the year to expect people to shell out £62 (£77 in Northern Ireland).

I think that it is not sufficient either to say that the best way to convince people of the value of broadcasting is through the programmes that one transmits. That is extremely important but people readily take that for granted. I think that there is a real task in engaging people in discussion, and debate, and in vigorously exposing the nature of the alternative. Perhaps we should suspend our programmes for two weeks and give the audience undiluted satellite material. Maybe this game is lost, but we prefer not to believe that. I prefer to believe that it is worth a candle, and that there is a sense that people want more from broadcasting, from television stations, than quiz shows and game shows and strip-shows which European satellite broadcasters are increasingly providing.

It is very difficult to engage the audience in ways which help them see the value of paying the licence fee. I think that there has to be a public relations approach, a concentrated marketing approach, as for a lot of other things. For example, is it worth more to you to have a broadcasting service which costs less than the Irish Times on a daily basis or less than any other newspaper, than not to have it? I don't know, it's a very difficult question. Sorry for going on.

Don Anderson: Independent Television Commission
Many of you may not have heard of the Independent Television Commission. It arose from the ashes of the Independent Broadcasting Authority and the Cable Authority and came into existence at midnight on the December 31st last. I would like to say I remember the occasion, I'm afraid I don't remember midnight of December 31st. That's as maybe. I was fascinated by a couple of themes in what I was hearing from the three speakers and I thought maybe all three of them were a little bit too defensive. I know that there has been ten years of Thatcherism and everything that that involved, but I am beginning to see, and I wonder if I am alone in this, I would be interested to hear what they think, I am beginning to see that the tide has indeed turned. I don't think that the fall of Mrs Thatcher was simply the fall of the leader of Thatcherism, I think part of Thatcherism fell with her. I would sound as evidence the passage of the 1990 Broadcasting Bill, then going through Parliament. This bill, you may remember, arose from a white paper which was written to all intents and purposes,

by the Department of Trade and Industry who saw broadcasting in terms of its commercial entity and little more. It was not seen as a cultural force.

It is interesting to see that in the committee stage, during the last autumn, that this was absolutely demolished, well perhaps not absolutely demolished but it was demolished in large parts, clause after clause, so what began as a process to erect a system with a 'light touch' has ended up anything but. What you have got now is a system that is still going to have the essential element of consortia having to bid for a station but the envelopes are only going to be opened, the money envelopes, after an examination of the quality of the programme proposal and that's quite important. How do you judge quality? I recollect your phrase, 'Its not a quality threshold but a quantity threshold.' This really demonstrates that you can judge a quality of programmes on two levels – one on the quality of schedules and the other is the quality of the programmes within the schedule. It is far easier to judge the quality of schedules, say to look at the range and see if it goes from children's programmes to sport, news, current affairs, drama what have you. It is of course going to be much more difficult to make a judgement as to what the quality of those individual programmes within that schedule is going to be. That's where, in the judgement of those bids, judging of this quality threshold, the ITC is going to be looking at the kinds of people who have been brought together. Is this a viable statement of programme quality given the kind of the people who are making them? Now that is actually going to be part of the quality threshold, it's quite important and it does mean that instead of a 'light touch', what you are going to have in the ITC is an organisation which can do a darn sight more than the IBA ever could.

The IBA could only finger wag a company or take the contract clause away completely. Those really were the two sanctions. The ITC will be able to start by finger wagging, go through private admonishment, then public and then a fine. It can reduce the term of the licence of some (its not a contract any more, its a licence) or it can actually withdraw the licence all together. So there is a range of actions that can be taken against companies who are reneging on their licence. When it comes to the licences, the programme promises that are made to get the bid will be written into the licence and become part of the licence document itself.

Now that's what actually arose out of the new proposals and there are people who believe that the tide has turned and the day of the institution, if you like and that includes broadcasting institutions, will actually see a resurgence. I will be interested to hear later what you think.

Michael Beattie

I would only make a brief comment in response to that, I would not dispute any of Don's speculations. When one talks about quality and quantity, any potential applicant must base his programme plan on his anticipation of income. So the financial future still dictates how far any one can go. If for example we decide to invest a vast amount of money in quality programmes, the financial side of your house may suggest to you the money just isn't going to be there for that. So finance still dictates to a very large degree for every potential contender what that programme plan will be.

Simon Woods: Northern Visions, Belfast

It is a question directed at Michael Beattie and Bob Collins. What is it about mainland or British organisations like Channel Four that makes them able to more effectively explore cultural complexity in the North of Ireland than UTV or RTE? It seems from the descriptions that we heard from the people at the top that that seems to be the case. Bob Collins seems to be putting forward a suggestion that the way broadcasting is going is that you have to combat the American style or line of approach to tv, possibly producing something like, I think somebody referred to it as Euro-pudding. Things like *Euro- Cops* explains that quite well. Whereas my feeling is that it is important to go for the regional variety which exists in Europe, like the documentaries that have been going out on Channel Four recently about the Soviet Union and Latvia and Lithuania and places. It seems also from the way people have been describing it that they are making a separation between the description of culture and cultural activity and the political forces that operate on them as broadcasters, when doing cultural work. For instance it interests me to know how UTV or RTE especially might be covering the 75th anniversary of the Easter Rising. It is quite a debate how to commemorate this, regardless of how it is done on tv. And this does have an effect, I got hit once because the BBC stopped broadcasting the Twelfth live and somebody assumed that I was from the BBC, (I found that quite insulting really). But I would like to know why it is that you have an organisation like Channel Four which is from outside, being able to make quite brave political decisions to cover areas of cultural diversity in the north of Ireland, particularly, which RTE and UTV seem to find politically difficult.

Bob Collins

Can I respond briefly to that? Your comment about the reaction to the American domination of television values suggests to me that I didn't make myself clear. I don't advocate the Euro-pudding or the *Euro-Cops* as a response to that. I am not suggesting that one should attempt to set up a counter Euro-approach to the American approach. What I was saying was that what is becoming dominant is the perception of television as being valueless, as not having a community role or a social role, as being purely a commodity which is traded and which has no purpose, function or responsibility beyond that. That is the American view which is becoming more dominant or more pervasive in Europe. It is against that view that I believe a stand has to be taken, not by way of Euro-pudding but by precisely what you say, indigenous and regional programmes which relate to the audience that is being served. This brings us to the second point. I don't see our principal purpose as being to make programmes which people outside Ireland will want to view. If they do it's a bonus. We are not principally in the business of selling programmes. If we can, we will. It is desirable that some programmes we make should be seen abroad but it is not the starting point. On the question of whether Channel Four is more courageous or more vigorous, or more innovative in its role, I think there is a two fold response. The first principal responsibility is to the audience which we were established to serve and our principal preoccupation has been that audience. I feel, as I have said earlier, that there is considerable room for us to develop ranges of programming specifically in relation to Northern Ireland and even more specifically within that in relation the representation of the unionist tradition within Northern Ireland.

I think the second undeniable situation is, *pace* Martin, finance. Channel Four may feel stretched at the moment in terms of its financial flexibility, but it has dramatically more revenue available than we have. If you take into account the range of material which we have to do to serve the immediate needs of the audience – news and current affairs whatever – the amount of money available with which to do other things or with which to commission an independent producer to do other things is very small indeed and that is not an inconsiderable element in the distinction. I think also Channel Four's remit from its inception was to do things differently, to make different kinds of programmes, to adopt a different approach than that which was adopted by the pre-existing national broadcasters in Britain. I think there is an element of that in relation to the differences between it and RTE in respect of Northern Ireland.

David Bailey: Independent Producer
I would like to take Don Anderson up on a couple of points he's made. The rather rosy picture that he painted about the powers of the newly-formed ITC in the next franchise round. Having been involved in the past in a franchise bid, I am curious to know about this whole question of quality, programme quality. I would like to ask Don, really in the next franchise round will paper promises of quality really mean anything more than they ever have done in the past and really, in effect, will it not be political and financial criteria that are all important? When he comes to talk about the powers of the ITC to finger wag programme companies, franchise holders, more effectively than in the past. Really, will that finger wagging be there for anything other than to finger wag at worries about sex and violence and inevitably political balance? Will it really be on the extraordinarily thorny issues of subjective view of quality of a programme?

Don Anderson
I feel like I am taking up too much of the time so I suppose really I should say I will reply in private but those are legitimate queries. Derek Bailey is well known as a producer of programmes of superb quality and that maybe is one way in which you can answer that question. If his name is behind a programme or programme proposal, then I for one, and many others, would feel that you have in that a guarantee of quality.

Derek Bailey
It wasn't good enough for the franchise last time round!

Don Anderson
I can say two things to that. One I wasn't there. Two, the system now is new, the quality threshold will probably be surpassed by more than one bidder. I would tend to think that quite a few people are going to spend, say a quarter of a million pounds, because that's what it's going to cost for anybody to apply say for the Northern Ireland licence, a minimum of that. If they are going to spend that you can be sure that they will put together proposals that, well I would imagine that they would put together proposals which will meet quality thresholds and they will have made the kind of proposals which most people in this room would consider satisfactory. But the bid of Thatcherism, which was not taken out of the round this time, and which wasn't there last time, comes after. How much money is in the envelope! There is not a thing that the ITC can do about that, except in exceptional circumstances.

James Hawthorne
I should like to explore a little more the issues raised by Martin's impeccable research within his extended family!

Suppose you ask the mass of viewers the question: 'Would you rather not have a licence system?' you will of course get the expected answer. People will always rather not pay. But suppose you put the question in a different form: 'Would you like television in these islands to be like American, Italian, Hong Kong television?' An informed answer would require experience of other systems but, in fact, anybody who comes back from abroad, of whatever social or intellectual level, is likely to tell you that television in these islands, with all its faults, is vastly superior to what he had to put up with elsewhere. That better quality, widely recognised, has not been achieved by accident and it is now about to be seriously threatened by the new order of competition. We have of course had competition in British television for years and it may have led to some restriction in particular areas of development but, on the whole, it has been beneficial. We have always had competition for *viewers* and that's been the system for three decades. Now, we are to introduce competition for *advertising and sponsorship* where programmes will have to demonstrate their competitive capacity to be efficient vehicles for selling consumer products to vast audiences. That seems to be the perfect invention for running down the quality of television as we know it.

You might challenge that with the argument that there are many distinguished television programmes made in America. We have access to the best of them but the majority of America's output is poor. There is of course the classic well-made American documentary which sponsors will rush to support – perhaps it will be about an expedition – some laudable hi-tech adventure – advertisers will like to be associated with a success story. But try to make a disturbing story about drugs, or inner-city decline, or inefficient administrations or crooked commercial practice and you'll find it virtually impossible to raise the money.

One of the best documentaries made by British television in recent years was Paul Hamann's *Ten Days in May* – I think that was its title – about the final prison days and the execution of a young black accused of a murder he was very unlikely to have committed – we now know that he certainly did not commit the murder. The film was shown in over thirty countries. In America it was not wanted by any of the big networks and when it was finally shown on so-called 'public television' it was cut down to half. That's the reality of competitive advertising and sponsorship.

Don Anderson has enunciated the important changes in the IBA/ITC rule book which will protect the interests of the viewer. But we had rules before and rarely was there the bottle to apply them. Take the beginning of TVAM. TVAM started out – and I quote – with 'a mission to explain' and with so resonant a phrase it won its franchise on the grounds that its promises were more high-minded than the others. What happened when it abandoned its ideals within a very short time of going on air? Answer: it was allowed to survive, it was allowed to forsake its stated principles. It was heading for financial collapse and then along came Roland Rat – the first time in history, said a cynic, that a rat saved a sinking ship.

Let me say, rather nearer to the bone, that Ulster Television's franchise will be challenged in this coming round. I don't know if there are any challengers present. I suspect challengers will be stronger in the grocery trade or some equally relevant commercial sector because that will be the flavour of the contest. But I do know of other serious contenders who by now may have abandoned their projects because they have been deterred by the commercial ambience and the unacceptable financial gamble.

Brian O'Kelly: Community Video

I am a resident of West Belfast. The terrorist community as it is sometimes labelled by the media. My experience of life in West Belfast is living within enclaves and closed boundaries. As a Catholic growing up in West Belfast I was told that by living at a given address I automatically became part of the main Catholic parish, which in turn is part of a certain Catholic diocese. As a voter I have a right to vote for an individual who as my councillor will represent me because I live within his or her ward. On another occasion I can vote for another individual who will claim to represent me because I live within his or her constituency. The media tells me that I live in West Belfast, in the troubled city of Belfast, Co Antrim, one of six, internationally referred to as Northern Ireland, some of my fellow inhabitants preferring Ulster, because despite the lack of three counties, that's their preference. My other fellow inhabitants will impress upon me that I live in the island of Ireland off the west coast of Europe and some powerful individuals via the media will refer to my European status, particularly from 1992. Green-minded folk, via the media, will advise me to act local and think global because of the valuable contribution I can make to Mother Planet Earth. All these have one thing in common, to a large degree they are externally imposed on me. My life experience involves living in certain houses in small streets. These local areas or districts have influenced me. I am proud of them and if I had been a country person I am sure certain townlands and villages and towns, a certain site may have attached themselves on my mentality. My statement to the media is – these places, these streets and houses are internalised by me, they are important. Hence I support community-based programmes such as those made by companies like Northern Visions to give my community and other communities a chance to have a good look at ourselves. There is a certain amount of feedback to us in those programmes which we relish and demand right of. There are some people who would say that that is rather subjective and by looking at ourselves all the time, we are in danger of disappearing up our own arse, so to put it. But I would rather disappear up my own arse than spend my life picking somebody else's, by making the programmes they think are marketable according to their criteria.

Bernice O'Donoghue: Irish Co-Op Films, Dublin

I would like to take up Bob Collin's point that public service broadcasting serves a community which is made up of interlocking minorities and that all of these should be represented. Fine words, but these don't mean very much as far as RTE is concerned. As long as Section 31 exists we can't talk about *all* communities being represented.

Secondly, I want to address the question of the communities of interest which you say RTE must serve. I would like to ask you what community you think you are serving because I don't believe that all communities of interest – working class communities or whatever – are represented adequately on RTE.

Furthermore, Rod Stoneman said that he thought independent producers have a finer sense of the complexities of certain issues or certain communities, than the institutional broadcaster often has. I would argue that RTE's record of commissioning programmes from independents is abysmal.

The fact that you don't represent communities adequately is clear from my own experience working on a film about the Whitefriars community in Dublin. RTE put money into it but subsequently when speaking to one of your staff I was informed that he considered that the programme was not worth screening. *Whitefriar Street Serenade* was made in co-operation with the local residents association and the people there felt that they were represented honestly and fairly. When I asked why it couldn't be shown this person's opinion was that it was too parochial and full of the old cliches about the rich and the poor. I never got that in writing though I asked for it.

Bob Collins

I didn't get the precise point but I certainly got your drift. Section 31, I don't defend section 31, I have consistently expressed my opposition to the existence of section 31, I believe that editorial decisions should be made by broadcasters and not imposed by governments and to that extent if you want to preface my remarks about interlocking minorities with the words 'apart, let's say, from the existence of section 31' please do so and you won't misconstrue me. On the other three points that you raised which are in some respect interconnected. In terms of defining the community we serve or the communities we serve, as I said earlier, principally we serve, we are there to serve the people who live in the state in which we are established. In addition to that we have always taken the view that we broadcast on this island, from this island and to as many people as can receive our programmes on this island. I never claimed that we are perfect or that we are not flawed, or that we have not failed adequately to represent certain communities, whether they be rural communities in some instances or urban working class communities in other instances or communities of opinion or communities of interest. What I was saying earlier was attempting to define what I believe to be the objectives which we should be seeking to attain. Fine words don't butter any parsnips but I think it is better to have a view of where one is going, even if one doesn't quite measure up to that, than to flounder around without it or than simply to absorb or to adapt the by now prevailing ethos in relation to the role of television. Maybe it is true, that's certainly your view and you are entitled to express it, that we have an abysmal record in relation to commissioning programmes from independent producers. I wouldn't describe it as abysmal, I wouldn't describe it as wonderful. I would describe it as, in the circumstances, not too bad. I would like it if we had more money. I would like it if we had more facilities to commission material which comes to us which is attractive, innovative and so on. We don't. I would like it if we could commission more fiction. I would like it if we could commission *any* fiction.

We operate within extremely limited resources. Without getting into the details of RTE's particular difficulties, a Bill was introduced and enacted within two months in 1990 which substantially limited RTE's revenue with effect from October. That's a real consideration; we had to reduce by 16 per cent the revenues we had available with which to commission programmes from independents. In relation to the *Whitefriar Street Serenade* your so far anonymous colleague of mine is probably not so anonymous, I think I recognise some of the turns of phrase. I think we could talk about that separately. I don't share the view that programmes which are about a small community shouldn't on that account be transmitted on a national channel. I don't take the view that anything that is made should be transmitted, but I take the view that most things that are made, subject to the quality should have a place in our schedules because we have two channels, we acquire a substantial amount of material from outside Ireland, we have a considerable amount of space to accommodate programmes which have been made in Ireland and I don't see a major difficulty in relation to transmitting programmes which are narrowly focused but good.

Simon Woods

We sent you six programmes ready to show, we have never received a reply even. (From RTE, not you personally.) We never even got a reply, 'Thank you for sending the tape', let alone show them. We don't want pots of money, they're made already. I don't understand what the difficulty is. It seems that it can only be a political difficulty or an organisational one.

Bob Collins

Well it may be an organisational difficulty but isn't a political difficulty. There is only one programme that I am aware of from Northern Ireland which we have not transmitted for political reasons, ie for section 31 reasons and that's *Mother Ireland*. But apart from section 31 I don't see any reason why we shouldn't transmit it. As they say in the Dail Eireann, I will communicate with the deputy.

Michael Beattie

I would like to make a very brief response to that and to the point from the gentleman who is in danger of disappearing where the sun doesn't shine. I speak as someone who has worked for a while in the BBC, who has worked as an independent and on a few occasions with Ulster Television. I can't dispute a lot of what you say, it has been my experience that to a certain degree, in certain areas there has been a cosiness and complacency and sense of comfort within the institutions, but that's not to deny that they have done some exploratory programmes from time to time and created complications from time to time with institutional authorities. All I can say is that it's my view that things have been slowly changing and are slowly changing, maybe not fast enough for you or fast enough for me but they are changing. In 1991 25 per cent of Ulster Television's output will be commissioned from independent producers. We can talk about that later, how that will actually help. Belfast Film Workshop for example will have material transmitted and Northern Visions will have one film transmitted soon. You will be aware that it was 3 months ago or there abouts when I first saw it, and I had to convince colleagues that it was worth showing. Eventually we got there and another one is on its way, so all I can say is, it is changing. It might not be changing terribly quickly but it is changing.

Desmond Bell
   I think we will probably have to blow the whistle there and thank our three speakers for their contribution. The day will of course continue after lunch and we look forward to seeing you all then.

SESSION 3

Chair – Des Cranston

Media Studies, UUC

Broadcasting in a Divided Community

Good afternoon and welcome back. Can I also say at this point how nice it is to see so many former students of media studies here, and indeed former students of the old institution NUU, from the days when you could combine degrees, Education, English and so on, with media studies. To see that so many former students are now gainfully employed is also very welcome. We also welcome Erasmus students. For those of you not involved with education, the Erasmus scheme is a European student exchange programme and the 1992 influence has arrived with us already. We have lots of young people from Holland, Spain, Italy, Germany, France and elsewhere, on the campus with us, breaking down many of the parochial, provincial barriers in our seminars. The local and the global, as it were, meeting in educational and social milieux.

We have four speakers this afternoon and I will introduce them collectively if I may. The first person to speak is David Butler. David was a student of Media Studies and he has now come back to teach here. His specialist research area is the peculiarities of British broadcasting in Northern Ireland.

The second speaker is Derek Bailey, who has already spoken this morning and has identified himself as a former challenger to UTV, but of course Derek started his broadcasting career in Ulster Television in the early 1960s and then went on to other things. In 1971 he was, of course, editor of *Aquarius* and he has vast European and co-production experience. His list of film awards is too long really to list here, but I should mention particularly the TV Arts Journalism Award which he won in 1987 and won again in 1990 for his film *Playing Belfast.*

The third speaker is Margo Harkin. Margo is a former member of the Derry Film and Video Workshop, or perhaps, a former member of the former Derry Film and Video Workshop – I am sure that will be clarified in a moment. She is of course the co-writer and director of *Hush-a-Bye Baby*.

And finally, but by no means least, we are delighted to have a radio person here. It was mentioned earlier how important radio is and we have Mickey McGowan from Radio Foyle, a station which I think contains some of the things that Rod Stoneman referred to this morning. It is something that is small and valuable although it is founded in some other institution. So I am very happy indeed to welcome the four speakers. I will not in any way try to define what they are going to say but again we will be picking up the discussion after they have finished. So first of all I call on David Butler.

f

DAVID BUTLER

Media Studies, UUC

I am used to lecturing in this room but not with a microphone so forgive me if I shout. Peculiarities is an oddly academic word – all I'm really talking about in this session is television in Northern Ireland. To do so we have to address its Britishness or otherwise and that seems to me to be the crux of the matter because it's very clear that, although nominally British, things here are, to put it mildly, different. I want to try to do some agenda setting. I'm sorry these points won't be fully developed in the short space of time available but I will summarise quickly what I'm going to do. In order to talk about the nature of broadcasting in Northern Ireland I first have to make some assertions about what I think the kind of mainland model entails, (I use that term advisedly – I think in this case it is apt). After making some comments on the British system I will then compare that with how I think it operates in Northern Ireland, given the peculiarities of society and politics in Northern Ireland. I will then finish off with a few preliminary comments about the problems of representation in Northern Ireland that are raised when broadcasting to a community in conflict. Hopefully that will lead also into the last session where we are talking about ways forward. So anyway that is more or less what I want to do, so first to say a few things about the British system.

Due to the need for brevity, these formulations may seem somewhat ahistorical and schematic. Nor is it possible to develop all the points as fully as I'd like. Apologies on both counts.

The British 'mainland' system of Public Service Broadcasting (PSB) is, I think it's fair to say, a 'consensus' model. Let me stress that the idea of an historic consensus in British politics and society is just that, it's an idea. It is, nonetheless, a powerfully influential idea. By convention, a state of consensus is said to exist where there is seen to be a 'general agreement between consenting parties' in the polity and society, and where, in spite of formal differences, the parties to that consensus 'share more things in common than they have separating them'. Much more than this, the ideal implies a sense of social harmony in the community at large. Politics in a 'consensus society' are supposedly undertaken 'on the basis of an already existing body of agreed opinions'. This harmony model (as it might be called)[1] thus presumes the existence of a reasonably homogenous and unified culture and society. It is above all an integrative model.

Flowing from this normative view, 'consensus broadcasting' is believed to represent perfectly a 'balance' of the various interests making up 'public opinion', always of course 'within the limits' of 'responsibility'. It is clear that since its inception in the 1920s, British PSB has been characterised by one constant feature – an attempt to maintain the (bogus) appearance of 'national unity', of oneness. Premised as it is on the 'production of consent' or at least common assent, for it's unitary outlook, the inclination to unify is built into the system – the inclination to unify is endemic to the system.

From this observation an obvious question arises: how can the harmony model be applied to a society which is evidently in a state of conflict; where the pretence of unity is untenable? Ours, after all, is plainly a society in which, for most of the time, all that the two communities share in common is a mutual antipathy.

My reading of the recent history of British television in Northern Ireland, suggests two ways of 'broadcasting to a community in conflict', (I'm talking specifically about the local broadcast media and about the period since the mid 1970s). The first of these strategies applies to local news and current affairs output – and I'd stress that I see it as a positive development. The policy shift was formally outlined in 1977. According to Richard Francis (Controller BBC-NI, 1972-80), by then it was apparent that:

> the BBC's credibility depends more on impartiality than balance, and our responsibility lies as much in reflecting the significant voices of the people, *including subversives*, as in sustaining institutions not wholly accepted.[2]

It's worth drawing out the implications of this emphatic revision of terms. The mainland model, we'll remember, presumes a reasonable centre of gravity in politics and society. But in the aberrantly dissensual circumstances of Northern Ireland, Francis continued, the concept of 'balance' was 'an over simplification'. Speaking on behalf of the institution of broadcasting, he argued that 'impartiality' could only be assured from outside Northern Ireland, in effect, by the Britishness of the broadcast system: 'It is the BBC's editorial policy unity which provides the essential stability in an often unstable environment'.

The duty of the broadcaster, in other words, was to act as an honest broker, guaranteeing impartial representation between the various 'relevant' forces in the polity – including Sinn Fein – thereby in so doing achieving a state of *balanced sectarianism*. The crucial point about this system is that it works against the integrative impulse – the tendency to unify – of the mainland model. It is effectively a system of dissensus broadcasting, which at the very least has the advantage of producing a more adequate appraisal of the balance of political forces in Northern Ireland than is permissible in Britain. Ironically, it is a form of imposed power sharing. I'd stress again that I see it as a positive development. I've said that this policy applies in the main to news and current affairs output, yet the most conspicuous success of balanced sectarianism is Radio Ulster's weekday news magazine *Talkback*. The programme reproduces a cross-section of terrifyingly sectarian reactions to a range of newsworthy issues. Enough to put one off one's cheese sandwiches, it is, though, fairly 'representative' of the fissured nature of public opinion in Northern Ireland. Mercifully, it does not attempt to manufacture a consensus where none exists. On the same basis, I'd wish to defend *The Show* as a noble failure. The idea was a good one. It's mistake was misjudging the moral conservatism of Northern Ireland civil society. Satirising politics was one thing, smut was quite another.

However, in contrast to the derring- do of the early editions of *The Show*, in most of the rest of their treatment of matters relating to culture and identity in Northern Ireland (and this is the second strategy I alluded to), the local broadcast agencies hark back to the idiocies of the pre-1968 policy, pretending all is sweetness and light and projecting a 'civic' culture of similarity by eliminating the divisive issues and by 'building up the centre ground'.[3] In real terms, this end is only achievable by sanitising sectarian culture. Presenting, in this manner, the Garvagh Sham Fight, traditional music and Irish dance, GAA games, St Patrick's night, Remembrance Sunday, the funeral of Thomas O'Fiach, and the Twelfth, as if they were ordinary public occasions requires an act of faith not unlike a child's belief in Santa Claus. This seems to me to be a less than appropriate response.

But of course there is a problem. How do we go about representing the 'cultural traditions' in Northern Ireland in ways which avoid de-politicising their seamier aspects? The core of it is that for (at least) the past twenty years civil and political life in Northern Ireland has been characterised by almost total division. Culture in Northern Ireland is sectarian. More than that cultural practices are the principal means of signalling and reinforcing existing divisions. Territoriality is all. Sectarian totems stake the boundaries between two mutually exclusive sign systems. We're all keenly aware of the differences between these symbols, and 'telling'[4] them apart can sometimes be a matter of life and death. All of us appreciate the difference between the pronunciation of the letter H as 'haitch' or 'aitch'. Nor can there be a settlement to the dispute, in either the political or cultural terrains, because both protagonists reject the legitimacy of the other's terms of reference. It comes as no particular surprise, therefore, that the politicians cannot get past 'talking about talks', for in this 'country' dialogue, political or cultural, is a near impossibility. And so long as the killing and structural inequalities continue, sadly, there can be no basis of consent, even over which proper nouns to use, (Northern Ireland, the north of Ireland, the North, Ulster, the six counties, the Province).

By the same token there can be no neutral language, verbal or visual, no uncontested images, and certainly no unifying imagery. Every signifier is spoken for. This, it seems to me, accounts for why the iconography of the Troubles is so stale and predictable. In one respect it is nobody's fault. The perpetual stand-off between Orange and Green orthodoxies not only obstructs feasibly non-sectarian formations from emerging, but it has also petrified political ideologies and cultural practices in outmoded seventeenth and nineteenth century (i.e. pre- or early modern) forms.[5] Reliance on cliche and second-hand motifs is nearly unavoidable, marring all but the most imaginative and critically-informed of representations. I'm not saying there aren't any points of cross-sectarian exchange, or instances of fruitful re-workings of basic thematic material *within* the respective 'traditions' – *Hush-a-Bye Baby* is one such critically informed and imaginative engagement with the terms of the nationalist discourse.

I, for one, think we've had quite enough banality and wishful thinking. No more folklore, please! There is no purpose served in deluding ourselves that this is anything other than a deeply fractured polity and society. The way forward, it seems to me, lies in representing in words and pictures the contradictions as they actually are, however ugly or irreconcilable. Better for all to realise what's going on around us than to make the mistake of mis-recognition, of mis-representation.

NOTES

1 See Keith Middlemas, *Politics in Industrial Society*, Andre Deutsch, London, 1979: especially chapters 8 and 14.

2 Lecture by Richard Francis, *Broadcasting to a Community in Conflict – the Experience in Northern Ireland*, at the Royal Institute of International Affairs, 22-2-77. Speaking in his capacity as Controller of the BBC-NI, Francis' views fairly reflected the corporate response to Roy Mason's strong-arm tactics.

3 For a description of the historical background see Rex Cathcart, *The Most Contrary Region*, Blackstaff, Belfast, 21984: chapter 6.

4 See Frank Burton, *The Politics of Legitimacy*, RKP, London, 1978: particularly part 2.

5 Roy Foster, *Modern Ireland, 1600-1972*, Penguin, London, 1989: 569.

DEREK BAILEY

Independent Producer

Good afternoon ladies and gentlemen. I am at this point in time fairly overwhelmed. I have just been making programmes for thirty years. Lecture theatres, media studies courses are foreign territory to me and coming in after the force of David Butler's argument, what I have to say really – in the course of those thirty years, not really having been privy to the councils of programme making policy, the committee rooms and board rooms, I have just been, as I have said pressing, on making the things – what I had prepared to say I have actually left behind in my case. Listening to the range of arguments this morning and the intellectual depth of the argument, I realise that my best contribution would be to make some comments simply as a practitioner, from my own experience of working in the field, both here and across the water. The placing of me immediately after David Butler is really rather harsh, Mr Chairman, I have to tell you, having been personally responsible for many of the pre-1968 'idiocies' in broadcasting and indeed, even today, still I guess in David Butler's eyes, perpetrating many of those 'idiocies'.

However I remain unashamed of that. The title of this session is Broadcasting to a Divided Community, in a divided community and already I can hear the rumble, I am quite sure. I wouldn't blame you if some of you were saying, what in the name of fortune does he know about broadcasting to a divided community as in fact he left this divided community precisely in the summer of 1969. Impeccable timing some may say. As it so happened, absolutely by chance.

Nonetheless I had been involved in broadcasting in the period from 1960 on and that, to us who were involved in broadcasting in those years, was a very exciting time to be involved and my goodness how naive we were! I think we genuinely felt that we were contributing to a better climate at the time. We *did* seem to be moving towards a greater sense of consensus, a greater sense of a joyful coming together, a greater sense of looking over the fence, of meeting up. Something of the naivety we were experiencing, may be evidenced by the fact that in 1965 we invented a late night current affairs programme and we give it the joyful title of *Flashpoint*. Had we known what was to come, maybe we would have thought twice, but we simply thought, well this is a wonderful idea and we can get all these opposing opinions in together and it will make wonderfully controversial television; and it did indeed. It went on live every night for at least half an hour, sometimes forty-five minutes, an hour after the News at Ten. I was appointed producer of the programme which was remarkable. As Michael Beattie was saying 'news and current affairs must be the core of any regional broadcasting'. Well, when I joined UTV in 1960 there wasn't a news programme, there wasn't even a current affairs programme, there was just something called a programme department.

There were one or two journalists and they chipped in their bit, but basically we were all programmers. Then the nightly news bulletin did come along, guided by such people as Robin Walsh, and gradually the news department became obviously more and more important. When I was asked to become producer of that nightly *Flashpoint* programme in 1965, certainly there was going to be a news element in it, but I remember very clearly that it became a constant battle between *us*, as we thought, the 'programme department', and *them*, the journalists, about the place that the increasingly evident, as Professor Welch has termed them, 'battalions of intolerance', who were on the march at the time, should have.

I, in my total naivety, was all for not giving these air time, but as it became news it had to be there and because it was there it had to be balanced and so the current affairs band- wagon got rolling – totally as I say to my distaste. Of course my distaste for it at the time was totally naive and came out of my own kind of protected idea of what life in the province was and should and could be about. In fact shortly after I left, in 1969, I was invited to come back and take part in a discussion programme. It was hosted by Kate Pratt, I remember, and there was a panel and members of the audience were allowed to chip in. I was horrified by how much oxygen of publicity had been given to the louder voices, the strident voices, the divisive voices, as I saw it and I said in my innocence at the time, that I felt broadcasting, and indeed here I agree with David

Butler, that the British model of broadcasting was totally inadequate to the needs of the province at the time.

I remember my very words because it was a) shortly after Phelim O'Neill had been kicked out of the Orange Order for attending a Catholic wedding and b) after there had been some further resistance by the Roman Catholic church to integrated education. I said on air, live at the time, I said that if the Orange Order does something that makes us look more anti-deluvian than ever, if the Roman Catholic church drags its feet on a measure that really would be to the good of this Province, then I feel that the broadcasters themselves should be in a position to actually say so. This is potentially a war situation, we are in a time of emergency, it's not good enough to sit back and let everybody have their voice. It's not good enough just to bring in the Pat Riddells and John D Stewarts as devil's advocates, as the voices of woolly liberals who because they are 'characters' nobody takes seriously. We the broadcasters should be editorialising in favour of a reduction in the things that divide us.

I remember Waldo Maguire, who was then Controller of BBC, saying to me, after more or less patting me on the head, 'Derek, well you know I really don't think it would work, I don't think so. I'm afraid we have to go on the way we are going.' So be it.

If I may draw on personal experience once again, so I did go away in 1970 and in 1971 I viewed from afar what had been happening, couldn't believe it and wanted to do something about it. I was in the fortunate position of being involved with a network arts programme at the time, *Aquarius*. I begged to be allowed the opportunity to go and make a documentary about my Belfast, 'The Other Belfast' and I was allowed to do that. I made the film that I set out to make, which was a film that was about the poets, the painters, the artists, about life in Belfast as I had experienced it. Of course what I didn't realise at the time, I thought I was making an apolitical programme, but of course the very fact of in those days, and the very fact now, of being apolitical about this place is obviously a highly political act in itself and I realise that.

The first realization of that began to dawn on me at that time. We spent, I think, ten days making that film and I brought a film crew with me from London and they said to me on the way down from the airport, 'Well Derek which lot are you?' I said, 'Well I am not going to tell you because to my mind if people stopped either asking that question or answering that question two or three centuries ago the place wouldn't be in the mess you see around you now.' And I added, 'You tell me at the end of the shoot, you tell me what you think I am, and then I will tell you.' So we had a marvellous ten days and they were completely baffled. We went to mass in St Mary's, we went to morning service in First Rosemary Street Presbyterian Church, we went up to the wonderful singing pub in Albert Street, where they were selling Long Kesh embroidered handkerchiefs as souvenirs. We went to the Linfield supporters club up the Shankill, where the Scots Guards had left their rifles in the cloakroom while they went in there to drink. We went up and down, across all the peace lines, the borders and barriers and so on and on the very last day they still didn't know. That morning we were filming outside the Arts Theatre in Botanic Avenue when I suddenly saw coming down for their morning cup of coffee, my eighty year old father and his sister, my aunt Eunice, tottering down to have their coffee in the Queens Espresso. I had been to see them during the week and I knew how depressed my father was that, being Belfast born and bred, all the certainties that he had leant on over his life, had been upended; the whole status quo had been called into question; how depressed and horrified he was. I thought, because I knew the camera crew had had a wonderful time, I really should introduce them to my father because he loved to think that people had come over from the mainland and had a good week. I said 'Oh father you must meet John Pike and his assistant, – they have had a good week here; haven't you Johnny?' Johnny was a Welsh man, and turned to my father and said 'Yes Mr Bailey, wonderful. Of course, I'm Welsh and I love all things Irish.' At which point my aunt turned herself into a fair imitation of a Giles grandma and brandished her umbrella and jumped up and down and said 'We're not Irish, we're British, we're British!' So my cover was blown; and I did go away thinking very deeply and very carefully about just what my view was and how apolitical I really was when it came to the bit.

The next time I came back to make a film about attitudes was an attempt to actually peel away those layers. I later did a film called *Family Ties* where I took six families and looked at them in depth through three generations to see if one really could shed or how far you could shed, the original sin of the attitudes and prejudices that you had inherited at birth.

If I can forget talking about the past and turn to Catherine O'Neill's point about why we can't project a better image or

project a non-violent image on the network, why did we never see
any programmes on the network that are about the *other* Belfast,
the sort of thing I attempted to do. It is very difficult because
frankly there is a terrible danger of those programmes, in network
eyes, being boring. Its very difficult indeed. I try all the time to find
the formula, to find a way. We did it to a certain extent with *Playing
Belfast*, which was a film about the Belfast Festival in the context of
the people who came to be in it, and I have recently been associated with BBC in Belfast and the outcome of that is a series which
is now ready for transmission, and I hope for the network and
that's called *Still Standing*. What I say about that is it is a series of
documentaries mainly by independent film makers here and its
not about the troubles and its not a whitewash, but it is about the
way in which people here have in the past, do now and will in the
future, work and play. I think they are exciting films but they are
about the ordinariness of life, or what the network may see as
being the ordinariness of life, and whether we get it on the
network or not I don't know, but believe me it is a real attempt.

Finally I would just like to say one final personal thing because
we do talk a great deal about news and current affairs. Michael
Beattie is saying that even in the hardest of times, with the financial pressures on, the one thing that is sure is that news and
current affairs do survive. I hope, I do hope, that more than that
just survives and as my guide to what broadcasting here for this
community and about this community should be I go back to the
broadcasters of the fifties – people of real vision working here in
the BBC. Ok, maybe the BBC itself was very establishment, very
Britain- orientated at the time, but they were people of real vision
who had a real sense of what broadcasting to this community
should be about. I've come across a book of Sam Hanna Bell's
written in 1951 to coincide with the Festival of Britain and I will
just quote these words, not only because of Sam, who was a great
broadcaster, but because he in turn quotes another great broadcaster, a great Ulsterman, W.R. Rodgers:

> We have with us still in Northern Ireland an antique conflict
> resolved long ago in Western Europe – the conflict of religious
> dogmas encrusted with loyalties, prejudices and racial aspira-
> tions. Yet, as W.R. Rodgers says, in *The Ulstermen and their Coun-
> try*, 'These characters, Protestants and Catholics are comple-
> mentary. They make two halves of life. One takes a long view of

life, the other a short and roundabout one. One is thoughtful and individual, the other is emotional and communal. It is this diversity and interplay of opposites that makes Ulster life such a rich and fascinating spectacle'. It might be added that it is this mingling, this whorl and eddy, driven by submarine currents, that make the surface of Ulster life such an intriguing perplexity to a stranger and the depth, such a vast imponderable to the Ulster artist.

Now I think that is a vastly greater challenge to broadcasters in this community than the sort of very depressing scenario – how we must simply look at the divisions – that David Butler puts forward. Thank you.

MARGO HARKIN

Independent Producer

I am here, along with Michael McGowan, to present a case history of a group which actually engaged in this whole idea of community programme making.

Derry Film and Video set up because Channel Four TV at that time had begun to make an intervention in the North of Ireland. The Channel did not have any in-house productions at all and commissioned all its work from outside. It advertised openly under its remit to cater for under-represented groups and regional voices and we leapt on that opportunity. We did so in the notion that perhaps a space had suddenly been created for people like ourselves who wouldn't normally have any opportunity to make programmes for all sorts of reasons that I really don't want to go into here. I think everyone here probably knows them very well. We saw that this opportunity had suddenly opened up but at the same time we were very cynical about the notion that there actually was a space there.

People have queried earlier how Channel Four, from the distance of London, could actually come in here and provide funding and enable people to make programmes from the kind of bases that we did. I think we ourselves suspected that it wasn't to do with a clear objectivity on their part and that they maybe didn't know exactly who we were. Under their remit however they were quite open to experimentation and we reckoned that we would try and get them to operate in that space for a while and see how it worked. We were trying to weigh up just how long it would be before we would be discovered, I suppose, but I have to say it didn't work out exactly like that because as always these things are never as simple as they appear in the beginning. They are always far more complex for both sets of people. It has to be said that Channel Four also quite deliberately engage in that space so our cynicism was a bit ill-founded and also, as the years went on, I think both of us were having to negotiate with the whole political situation as events actually unfolded.

When we set up in 1984 we had a few programme ideas, one of which was *Mother Ireland*. I am here to talk specifically about *Hush-a-Bye Baby* but it is important for me to refer to *Mother Ireland* because it was a documentary and it was the first broadcast-quality programme we made and the first documentary that we know of which suffered directly under the Hurd ban, as it became known. Because it was banned nobody ever really has been able to engage with the ideas that were discussed in that programme because any discussion in connection with *Mother Ireland* from that point on was always about its being censored. It has obviously been discussed in certain circles but not in the way that we had hoped it would if it had got on TV where it would be engaging a much wider audience that wouldn't necessarily know what it was tuning into.

Television was a very exciting notion for us in that it had the potential to get to people that we wouldn't be able to speak to otherwise. I know what I am describing here has often been called propaganda but, as we looked at it, we had watched for years how our lives had been represented on TV by programme makers from outside, and also from within where there was a great deal of self-censorship. I'm not just talking about news and current affairs because censorship there is very obvious, maybe not to everyone but certainly to us, and I can give you a brief example of this. When the people in Derry who had been present at Bloody Sunday went home that night and watched how it was reported on TV they just couldn't believe the sort of things that were being said in comparison to the experience they had had just been through. So since that point, and earlier I suppose for some people, there has always been a great cynicism about how events are reported.

However, apart from the documentary and current affairs coverage we also began to explore how fiction about Ireland had been discussed or historically how it had been contributed to, which was generally, again, by people from out of the country. *The Quiet Man* was one we discussed quite a lot because Ann (Crilly) wanted to include it originally in *Mother Ireland* and I remember hearing you Martin (McLoone) talk about it in Dublin. We began to engage with these kind of ideas, with how people outside actually portrayed you and the notion of stereotypes and so all these themes were discussed in the workshop.

I want to say, therefore, that making *Hush-a-Bye Baby* is a disappointment for me in one sense in that it could not be judged in relation to *Mother Ireland*. Some people make the connections because they have seen both programmes. I feel that they were part of a process, that one followed on from the other and although they are quite different in the way they deal with their particular themes I feel that in *Hush-a-Bye Baby* I was drawing out some of the things that had been brought up in the documentary *Mother Ireland*.

I just want to divert here to make a point about the relative power of both documentary and fiction. Different schools of thought hold the view that one is better than the other. I actually think that each of them is of equal importance. There is a notion that perhaps fiction is in some way an alternative to documentary while censorship exists. I don't think that fiction should be seen to be in service to censorship. I think it is a medium that has its own particular built-in qualities which enable certain things to be said, and I also think there is nothing to beat hearing and seeing, face to face on TV, people whom you might not normally meet, or who have a completely different point of view from you, telling you what they think.

But the reason for doing *Hush-a-Bye Baby* in fiction was because the subject matter itself was extremely sensitive. In 1983, before the group set up, we had had the abortion referendum in Ireland which was highly controversial. Myself and other members of Derry Film and Video had been involved in the debates around abortion and there were people, and I include myself here, who could barely speak because of their anger and it was difficult at times to articulate a reasoned point of view. Debate on the issue just split down the middle. You were either for it or against it and so it was an issue that I thought ought to be properly tackled in media.

I had seen some ways in which it had been dealt with before, such as in RTE's *The Womans Programme* which was an excellent series that's now gone, unfortunately. It did a programme about abortion but women who came forward to speak about their personal experience of abortion would only do so if they were silhouetted in the way that other programmes dealing with criminal issues silhouetted their interviewees. I felt that that criminalised the people who were trying to express why they chose to have an abortion. In the few cases where some very courageous women decided to talk up front to camera the boldness and energy required to do that perhaps antagonised people also.

So it was a very conscious decision to make *Hush-a-Bye Baby* as a fiction for all those reasons and to use the element of humour to take the sting out of the pain and anger of discussing that particular issue. A clear thrust of it was that we were trying to engage with people on this island. It was not meant for consumption in Britain. That's not to say that we don't think that it has a place there because clearly it does, but I knew that all the themes and notions and ideas that are woven through it would be recognisable to people in Ireland. We ourselves were having these discussions during the writing of the script and while making the programme and so we obviously wished that when it was finished it would engage other people. *Hush-a-Bye Baby* was the first programme where that process happened from beginning to end because, as I said, *Mother Ireland* was banned.

When we started making it there were different ways in which we had to negotiate with our so called community. The word 'community' gets used in all kinds of ways and I know it has been analysed before. Ever since Margaret Thatcher described the Poll Tax as the Community Charge its meaning has been devalued. I don't think that we necessarily believed that as a community organization we were representing a set of unimpeachable truths. I think Martin's (McLoone) word 'flux' describes very well what we were reflecting. For example when we were dealing with issues of gender there was a community of women who obviously had a particular point of view that we wished to reflect.

There were women who were going in their thousands each year to England to have abortions and yet their point of view was never, or rarely, discussed. The women who couldn't make that kind of choice, (because they couldn't get the information or they just couldn't bring themselves to do it because of their Catholic or Protestant upbringing), sometimes committed infanticide.

In this country we think that if we ignore the problem women will have their babies and everything will be fine. I don't know the figures for infanticide, and I suspect they are inadequate anyway since quite often its discovery is accidental, but it seems to me that they are quite high. In conducting my research I noticed quite often that the means people used to kill their babies was drowning. Again, not long before we started filming, a baby was washed up at Culmore Point in Derry. The case which most of you will know about is the story of the Cahirciveen baby which was washed up in a fertilizer bag on a beach in Co Kerry and it had been stabbed twenty-eight times. I became obsessed with it, knowing that somewhere there is the mother and father of that child and they are suffering this national controversy, and there are so many people suffering in similar agony.

As you know Joanne Hayes was falsely accused of the murder of the Cahirciveen baby and the tribunal of the case which she took against the Gardai turned into a trial of her and her moral behaviour. The judge virtually said that she killed her own baby which she had buried in a ditch following its death at birth.

The other main case that concerned me was that of Ann Lovett who was a fifteen year old girl who died after giving birth in a field next to a grotto of the Virgin Mary in Co Westmeath on 31st January 1984. Her baby died also and her fourteen year old sister committed suicide shortly after. The circumstances surrounding that case were all hushed up and I know that these things are very sensitive and difficult to talk about but I think it is atrocious that a fifteen year old girl should die giving birth. So these were the reasons why we wished to explore this particular idea.

When the film was being researched we had to negotiate with people in our community, with women whose stories we eventually told in a different way in the film and with the Catholic Church because we had to do research interviews and use some of its property.

Afterwards when the film was made we had this big night in Derry where all the people who had been involved or connected with it in someway, ie our families and friends, came along to see it. It was a fantastic night, we had a great reception, and afterwards I breathed a great sigh of relief because it seemed to appeal to people and everyone was very high coming out of it. Then the film went on the festival circuit where people chose to go and see it and it got really good reviews and praise and began to pick up awards.

But I began to get an inkling of what was going to come when I tried to put it on in the Hall Cinema in Derry, which is a small cinema run by the local Catholic Church. I wrote to Father Michael Collins whose church we'd used when we were filming. There is nothing kind of deprecatory about those particular scenes but obviously there is a criticism in the film of the Church which I think is very gentle really, considering. Anyway he asked to see a tape of the film which I supplied to him and he said he would let me know. This is a cinema which was showing films like *Blue Velvet,* *Dangerous Liaisons* and others like that. Father Collins wrote back declining to show *Hush-a-Bye Baby* in his main programme because of what he described as its 'unsympathetic spiritual treatment' which he believed rendered it uncommercial! He wondered if it was deliberate, which made me realise that he thought he was speaking to me as one of his parishioners and not as a client who wished to have a programme shown in his cinema. He gave a detailed review of the film which fluctuated between flattery and disdain, concluding again that I had shot myself in the foot commercially. This has clearly proved not to be the case. The film would have been highly commercial in Derry and in fact people have not understood why they didn't see it in the cinema. It seemed we were being held hostage, in a sense, by one element of the community that we came out of. That was the beginning of the kind of feedback we started to get.

Later on when it was shown on RTE we got a splurge of reaction to the film. People started to write letters to the local paper in the following vein:

If sewage is a part of any community then *Hush-a-Bye Baby* is a septic tank . . . the film seemed to condone the holocaust of abortion while the undignified behaviour of protagonists in making the drama scandalised both themselves and the people who finance such scatology. Signed: 'Average Punter'. (letters to the Editor, *The Derry Journal*, 28th September, 1990)

There are several letters in the same vein, referring mainly to the language, the nudity and the British soldier scene. There was a preoccupation about the bad impression that was conveyed of Derry to the outside world, particularly to the English. On another level there was a worry about how Protestants would perceive us now that this image had got out and we weren't projecting the image of Dana or that corporate video about Derry.

We had a lot of hate phone calls to the office, some of which were absurd. Geraldine happened to be on her own the day after the screening when the calls came. One woman actually lost the run of herself and complained that '. . . the language was a fucking disgrace'!

The important thing I should say is that the initial criticism of the film came from what was perceived as a section of the broader republican community and then it spread rapidly into the broader nationalist community. We didn't take up the debate because Derry Film and Video Workshop had already ended due to the fact that Channel Four had withdrawn our funding. The people then in the very same communities referred to earlier took on the issue of defending the film and did so publicly, sometimes without me even knowing about it. For example someone phoned me one day to tell me there was a radio discussion happening that moment on *Hush-a-Bye Baby*. I tuned in to Kate O'Halloran's afternoon programme on Radio Foyle and heard these amazing calls being relayed via the producer to Mary Nelis and a couple of young women in the studio who were talking about the film and defending it. Again they were getting ludicrous comments. One woman referred to the gratuitous nude scene in the film and it turned out to be the scene where the girl vomits in the bath. Mary Nelis pointed out that you do have to take your clothes off to take a bath.

So it was interesting that the film was not so extreme that people could switch off from it. It actually hit people in a way, and although obviously a lot of criticism of the film was probably filtered on its way to me I did hear that it caused quite a lot of discussion throughout Ireland. I heard that it was talked about the next day in hairdressers, at wakes, and in factories. People seemed to either love it or hate it but nevertheless it got discussed and I felt that that was proof in itself that something important happened.

MICHAEL MCGOWAN

BBC Radio Foyle

Before I start, I would just like to say one thing. When Rod Stoneman was standing here he said that had he been a member of the BBC he would have worn a tie and apologised then for not wearing one. I happen to be a member of the BBC but that is not the reason why I am wearing a tie. I happened to be brought up to wear a tie whenever I was meeting strangers and I think that's quite germane to the theme of all of today's discussion. I am going to make no apology what so ever for addressing myself to my notes. I am going to stick literally by them because in this kind of society, particularly in the kind of society that Radio Foyle attempts to serve, words cost lives.

I want to talk first of all about Derry, and immediately having used that term I have set myself up in your eyes, and in your ears, as someone coming from a certain tradition. I will not say which. Those are the kind of mental and cultural mind-sets that people engage in here, day in day out, and have engaged in them for the past 25 years.

Derry is a place with a long and proud history and an equally long and proud memory. It is a city with a split personality and that split personality can only be explained by the way in which the city's past comes back to haunt its present and it is this dialectic which continues to shape its future. Today it is seen as the North's second city but it was historically the first city and very definitively the first city of the 'Troubles'. It is a place where the word *patriotism* has two totally different connotations and it's the interpretation of this concept which forms the very basis of any sense of cultural identity held by one or other side. It was a plantation town which, to all intents and purposes, has been re-colonised by the natives. In an unique way, Derry, independently of the rest of Northern Ireland, it has been argued, is going through a post-colonial experience. This phase, and it's really only beginning, is evidenced by the fact that the city is attempting to come to terms culturally with its past. For instance, and it's an important for instance, for the first time last year, on a cold rainy summer's evening, the city's Guildhall Square was packed with people who braved the elements to watch and share in an event which, up until that point, had been the exclusive and triumphal property of the loyalist people of the city. For the first time in the history of the city an historically informed Catholic population was prepared to view a Siege Pageant as part of its shared heritage with the Protestants of the city. The seed for that evening in Guildhall Square had been sown a decade earlier with the City Council which had adopted a pioneering attitude towards its sponsorship of the arts – a major part of that was the setting up of the now internationally-re-nowned Orchard Gallery. It made the city into the Gallery and began to ask the most fundamental questions, as all significant art should, about the nature of the city and its inhabitants. It has been responsible for beginning an open, at times violent, cultural dia-logue within the city which would have been undreamt of twenty years ago. The difficulty, or more correctly, the paradox created by this kind of open dialogue was that in the case of the Siege Pageant, it was an event closed to the Protestant population of the city purely and simply because the majority of them chose to see it as a dialogue which challenged their received wisdom and which was politically inspired by a nationalist council. It was a dialogue which, if carried through to its natural conclusion, they saw as being antipathetic to their cultural tradition and one which they would have no part of. It was no accident that few, if any Protes-tants, were present that evening in Guildhall Square.

There are other, less cultural, reasons why the Protestant popu-lation was conspicuous by its absence that night – fear and suspi-cion and the ultimate and real threat posed by over twenty years of nationalist-inspired violence against the state which they were responsible for shaping. In today's Londonderry the price that Unionists have had to pay for fifty years of mis-rule is one of dispossession – they have been dispossessed of political power and because of twenty years of sectarian violence and intimidation they have been forced to consolidate their position on the East Bank. They are isolated and alienated by forces at play both inside and outside the Maiden City. The fact that, as they see it, the architect of the Anglo-Irish Agreement is a native of the city does little to allay these feelings of isolation and alienation. The fact that the

British government went over their heads when they signed this international agreement only adds to a belief that their sovereign government has betrayed them as settlers in what has become their homeland. They, in their own words, 'have been sold out' and Margaret Thatcher, one of the signatories of the latest attempt to resolve the Northern Ireland problem has been equated with Lord Lundy of old. Their allegiance now is to the monarch who is merely the symbolic head of state which they feel disenfranchised from and threatened by.

Protestant fears have not be assuaged by the reality of life in Derry over the past two decades. In the past twenty years, thirteen thousand protestants have uprooted themselves from the West of the city and resettled on the East Bank of the River Foyle. The three thousand who remain, so the graffiti tells us in the Fountain Estate, are not prepared to surrender – like their besieged antecedents. What we have, then, both politically and physically is an extremely polarised society. Such is the suspicion and perceived threat on the part of the Protestant population that I know of many East Bank Loyalists who have not been across the Craigavon Bridge to shop in twenty years. They regard the city side as simply bandit country and feel they would be better off if the two bridges connecting the East and West bank were dismantled thus leaving them in Northern Ireland and the nationalist community where it belongs – in the Republic. It's an attractive solution in many ways but it does nothing to solve their crisis of identity.

So what does all this have to do with Radio Foyle? The difficulty with Radio Foyle is that it was cast into the middle of that. I remember going for an interview to be employed as a producer in Radio Foyle about five years ago and I went through the interview and it was nice, it was dandy, it was valueless as far as I was concerned until it came to the pat point at the end of most interviews where you are asked if you have any questions. My first question was that I was surprised in this kind of company that I hadn't been asked what I think of the preconceptions of the Protestant community of the radio station, so they said, 'Well we haven't been asked but you ask it and you answer it. What would you do, how would you solve the problem?' My answer to that was that I would build a pontoon bridge in the Foyle and I would site Radio Foyle in the centre of it. In that way you are annoying and insulting no one. Which brings me now to the metaphor which is what Radio Foyle has become.

Ten years ago the BBC decided to establish a local radio station in the middle of this divided community – a community where the debates going on *within* the Nationalist community were just as important as those going on between Unionist and Nationalist. The station was to act as an honest broker both within and across the communities.

The nationalist community was suspicious of the station because it was financed by the *British* Broadcasting Corporation and the Unionist population was suspicious because it was sited on the nationalist West Bank. This suspicion was further fuelled by the fact that BBC Radio Foyle referred to the city as Derry, whereas the more extreme Unionist elements insisted that the station honour the city's Royal Charter and refer to it as Londonderry. Because the use of the name Londonderry was seen to be politically divisive (i.e. favouring one political tradition at the expense of the other) and because most of the local population on both sides of the divide used the name Derry in everyday conversation, it was decided to refer to the city as Derry. This rationale did little to assuage the fears of prominent Unionist politicians at the time who began referring to Radio Foyle in the local press as Vatican Radio.

As an aside, as far as the wider BBC is concerned, when it comes to the name of the city, on first mention it has to be referred to as Londonderry and thereafter as Derry. This approach might appear to be eminently reasonable, given the sensitivities of the audience, but that kind of rule has given rise to serious cultural anomalies when adhered to by the letter in the past, e.g. the Radio Times caption 'County Londonderry Gaelic Football Team'.

Those are the kind of subtleties that Radio Foyle is dealing with day in, day out. The difference between Radio Foyle and everyone else who has spoken here are the kinds of jobs that they engage in be it as BBC, UTV, or independent producers for television. The difference is that you make your programme and you go. It might be three or four months, maybe three or four years before your vision or your analysis or your reflection of society comes back on screen. The difficulty for Radio Foyle is that we can't cut and run. We are there. We are part of the community; we broadcast day in, day out; we are a speech-based public broadcasting unit sitting on the West Bank of the Foyle, therefore the difficulties which everyone has talked about here today are visited upon us 365 days of the year. Not for one hour.

So here in the name of the city was the first dilemma for this new station and the decision to use the term Derry, for the reasons I've outlined, still continues to cause difficulties for the station locally.

The issue of the most appropriate use of the city's name serves only to highlight the whole question of how Radio Foyle could fairly and equitably reflect and analyse the cultural traditions in the area and still strike a balance in its coverage of the concerns of the people of the North-West. In this extremely polarised society you had two communities who held opposing cultural, religious and political aspirations. The nationalist, and exclusively Catholic majority community associated very strongly with the County of Donegal, across the border, and the ultimate goal of a United Ireland. The Unionist and exclusively Protestant community looked in the opposite direction, towards the East and Belfast and ultimately to London for the maintenance of political union between Britain and Ulster. So how do you strike a balance in the context of this kind of society? But perhaps this is the wrong question? Perhaps a more meaningful approach to public service broadcasting in that kind of context would simply be to examine, analyse and reflect the two traditions and what it is that makes those two traditions distinctive and, more importantly, to make them mutually intelligible – the one to the other. That is exactly what Radio Foyle has attempted to do in the past eleven years. It is that very lack of perspective between the communities which has become the corner stone of any meaningful broadcasting that the station has engaged in. Had that not been the case the station would have ended up portraying a false reality or, worse still, ignoring the cultural and political differences which had given rise to the contradictions in the city in the first place. The station's commitment to that kind of ideal has to be total and it requires that the station be fair and impartial in its analysis otherwise what the station will achieve, if its not careful, is a reinforcement of the already existing prejudices. However, no matter how careful the station's programme makers are, that danger will always exist.

What has to be remembered in all of this is that Radio Foyle is sited on the West Bank of the Foyle on the predominantly nationalist side of the city. The difficulty here is that the station is therefore more easily accessible to that section of the community and therefore could develop a tendency to give pre-eminence to the cultural, social, economic and political concerns of the majority Catholic community. That ready accessibility has made the

station very much part of their way of life. How does the station
begin to reflect the concerns of the people on the other side of the
river if many of them see Radio Foyle's location as bandit territory
– no matter how ill – or well-founded that attitude may be?

The answer to that question is that the station has to engage
more pro-actively with that community because it has a duty to
reflect their concerns as well. The station seems to be getting it
right because according to the last, and most comprehensive
survey done on the public's attitudes towards the station, 88% of
listeners, and they come from both sides of the political divide,
said that they felt that Radio Foyle was part of the North West's way
of life now. The station has a weekly reach of 52% of the potential
audience, in other words 52% of the potential audience say that
they listen to Radio Foyle. Again the survey showed that Radio
Foyle was reaching into both communities.

One of the main reasons for the ability of the station to reach
into and across the communities is that the people who present
and make programmes on Radio Foyle are in the main from the
area and from both sides of the political divide therefore the
duologue which goes on in our programming continues on daily
behind the scenes. In that sense the programme makers have a
vested interest in getting the balance within and across programmes
right. It was a deliberate decision, from day one of the station's
existence, to have people from the area make programmes about
the area in which they lived – so for the first time people from the
area were in control of how they portrayed and analysed their own
town.

The local idiom became the language of the station, the two
communities concerns became the concerns of the station – warts
and all! There is not a day that goes by that does not give us food
for thought and each day we learn something new. The station,
eleven years on, is still a very delicate embryo, which could abort at
any moment. As a public service community radio station it still
continues to tread the extremely thin line between being *part* of
the community and remaining *apart* from it. And it has to remain
apart to maintain its editorial independence. The delicacy of this
high wire act, and the daily difficulties of attempting to reconcile
the irreconcilable aspirations of the station's audiences, are well
summed up by a casual remark made to one of the station's
presenters in a live phone-in competition during the qualifying
rounds to last summer's World Cup. The Republic of Ireland was

playing Northern Ireland in Dublin. The caller answered when asked harmlessly how the match was going 'Isn't it great. We're winning!' The Republic, by the way, had just scored. I knew, without a doubt, where her allegiances lay and immediately asked myself the question 'What would the Unionist audience, listening to that programme, think of a station which allowed such people such open and free access to the airwaves?!' I'm afraid that's the price your pay for adopting an honest approach to your audience. Thank you.

DISCUSSION

Professor Welch

The first thing that I want to lead off with is a comment on David Butler's notion that all the signifiers are spoken for which is actually a very bleak interpretation of the possibilities. All the signifiers are all spoken for, only if one allows them to be so. The whole point, I thought, about today's dialogue is that you *can* move the signifiers or move the understanding away from fixed positions. The next point I want to make is a linguistic one, a link between the two words, *responsibility* (and of course *impartiality* is related to that) and the word *response*. If there is a response to a situation, whatever the complexity of that situation, if it is a real response, it involves responsibility. Micky McGowan's paper was a superb example of how somebody with a very responsible job to do tries to chart his way between the different responses so that there is a link between response and responsibility and that link is something that is negotiated every time, every time a programme is made I would guess. Just as that link is made every time a piece of fiction or poem is created if it is a true piece of writing, if it's a serious piece of work, if it is a serious attempt at addressing the ways that images can shape our lives or take us over. Always there will be that element of responsibility, that element of negotiation, that element of trying to construct a way through what may be the mine-field of the different points of view. To give up on the enterprise and say all there is is division is I think a very bleak view. Now I understand David's strategy and I respect it, completely respect it, but David's strategy, his approach, is one which emphasizes the division. Once you move beyond that emphasis and try to construct for yourself an argument, a piece of writing, a poem or play or, I guess, a TV programme, responsibility comes into the question, that's if you are not going to give the lie to your responses. Response involves things like impartiality. I think it is a bit too easy sometimes, the way that impartiality and the idea of responsibility is thrown out of the window. So on that slightly querulous note, I will stop and yet congratulate all four speakers, on the way they addressed the question.

Tom Lovett: University of Ulster, Jordanstown

Yes I was quite taken by David Butler's point about Northern Ireland, that all the communities have in common is their antipathy towards each other. I thought that was a good, striking point about the situation and on the other hand I think he was quite right to argue that the alternative then is a lot of bland TV and video programmes which tries to tell us how much we all have in common. There is an alternative which in some cases I think Margo touched upon in what she has done in Derry. This reminds me when I worked in Derry, for eight years before we had the palatial studio we have now. We had two rooms, I think, in Strand Road in those days. We were commissioned by Radio Ulster to make a series that ended up as thirty fifteen-minute programmes about communities in Northern Ireland. We went round, not just the people in Derry but in Belfast, Omagh, all over the place talking to them about the problems that Margo has referred to in her film – the cultural changes that were taking place in their lives, the social and economic problems that they faced. All it indicated was that, going back to our speaker earlier this morning, people in Northern Ireland are engaged in a complex culture, a complex series of communities. They are struggling to *make* their community, they are struggling to *make* their culture. It's a positive act, there are a lot of contradictions in it and there are a lot of tensions, particularly for the Protestant community because it often means they are facing up against the State and they don't like that. In the end of these programmes we also went and looked at what are the differences because the message that came across from all these Protestants and Catholics, and they were Protestants and Catholics predominantly from working class communities, was they thought they had a great deal in common. 'We are the same sort of people.' They said it not me. We went on to look at what they have in difference. How did they see each other? And they did see each other quite differently and have to live with that and of course the job I think of those in the media is to marry that to some form of education. We tried to, in the sense of having discussion groups on the programmes and material to support it. I would have thought that is the direction. You have to take up the difference. There is a great deal of talk, I think, at the

moment in Northern Ireland about education for mutual understanding, cultural traditions, cultural heritage. Yet if you talk to
people in the field about that definition of community or culture it
means people struggling with the problems that beset them in every
day life. They can't see it, my experience is they can't see it. I think
that's the challenge.

Michael McGowan

Well, I would just say one thing. I think that point of view is an
important one and in that context the broadcaster, I feel, does
have a responsibility when it comes to an examination of the
different cultural traditions here. In terms of education, particularly in the field of education for mutual understanding, broadcasters have to do literally what the word education means – they
have to lead or bring people out – and lay bare our cultural pasts
and present. I think that this is an honest approach in a place like
Northern Ireland. There is a sense in which some people involved
in things like education for mutual understanding promote the
idea that we here have more in common than separates us. I think
the reality is that there is a lot of separation between the two
communities, both politically and culturally, otherwise, as a broadcaster, I have difficulty even beginning to explain what's going on
in Northern Ireland. It is an examination of this cultural separation which should form, for the present, the corner-stone of any
meaningful broadcasting. Now, in programming terms, once you
define, or at least force, people into a position where they begin to
question the received wisdom of their own side then I think you
have taken the first step on the road of examining, in a critical
fashion, the true significance of your own cultural tradition and its
place in this society.

In this context I think Radio Foyle is uniquely placed in that, as
I see it, at times it is serving a city which is the alter-ego of Northern
Ireland. What you have is a predominantly nationalist and Catholic society with a different value system and cultural mind-set from
the rest of Northern Ireland and it is an examination of these
settled values which is one of the corner-stones of the station's
programming.

Desmond Bell

I have certain reservations about Michael McGowan's contribution. Let me speak for that Protestant voice in Derry and say that

what he said about Derry Protestants is in many regards, a travesty of what the situation in Derry is – in its complexity, the complexity of those voices that can be heard and the confusions of those voices.

The first point I would want to make is that you are not accurate about the Siege Pageant. As a sociologist who has recently completed a research project on Protestant youth culture in Derry, I was going around the Guildhall Square trying to spot all the Protestants. I can assure you that there were lots of loyalists there on that particular night, completely interested in the historical dimensions. Those who have taken the most active role in loyalist demonstrations over the years in particular, went precisely to see how the other side did it. Perhaps cynically, yes, and with all sorts of reservations, but they did go along. Hence there was some sort of interchange.

Secondly, your perceptions of mobility in the city seemed to be very misplaced and not based on the sorts of social science evidence which are available, particularly towards young people. Certainly differences exist but there is a lot more mobility across the river than you suggest.

More seriously, though, is your presumption to speak for that community instead of actually releasing those voices and letting those communities speak for themselves. We hear somebody, albeit dealing with the conflicts, nonetheless speaking for the community as if it were completely mute itself.

I also find it very difficult (and I know a number of other people with a similar background as mine, West Bank Derry Protestants, fully at ease in, say, Donegal and conversant with Irish culture would agree) I find it very difficult to take your freezing and ghettoising of the divisions. Those divisions did not always exist as any number of historical studies show, including for example, Conor Doakes' superb study *Riots and Civil Strife in the City of Londonderry in the Nineteenth Century*. What my own film *Redeeming History* tried to show is that by looking historically at those divisions you describe, especially that period when they did not exist, by looking at the past, you can see the possibilities for the future.

The fifteen years or so which have led to the present divide as you describe it, *are* only fifteen years. In fifteen years time perhaps things will be different – they could be different. Again, talking about the significations being frozen for ever. I wouldn't accept that – there is openness and I am rather worried that as broadcasters and film makers we have actually reinforced those significations rather than as Bob Welch has said, challenged them. That's our responsibility – not to accept but to challenge them.

Michael McGowan

First of all, I think that I did not, and do not, speak on behalf of the people of Derry or Londonderry. If I thought I did I should start thinking of becoming a politician and forget about making programmes. What I was involved in was a personal analysis of the situation in Derry – an analysis from the extremes if you like – but a personal analysis nonetheless. If it gives rise to an extreme reaction from Desmond Bell I can understand that. I could have stood at the lectern and given a totally different analysis which would have been acceptable to everyone in this room but I chose not to. I chose to go out on a limb, to get people to at least begin to ask questions about the cultural traditions which inhabit this island and the area that Radio Foyle broadcasts to. I think that, as a broadcaster, if you do not go out on a limb, what you engage in is bland programming firstly and secondly there's the danger of visiting back on people the comfort of their own position. I think ours is a valid approach. That's the approach of Radio Foyle's programme maker's thinking – there's nothing frozen in that approach – in fact it's very fluid.

Tony Rowe

I was interested in David Butler's piece. I found it nicely provoking and at the same time there seems to be a dichotomy there where you were suggesting that, certainly, one should show the divisions and . . .

David Butler

The word I used was *contradiction*. There is a difference between contradiction and a division.

Tony Rowe

But it seems to me you are implying that *The Show* which to me appears to be showing those contradictions, had failed because it exposed the Northern Irish to their prudery. There was a line to cut off between sectarian and political divisions and suddenly there was a social morality or something – a prudery which suddenly made it fail. I don't quite know where the cut off line is, I am not sure whether the smut was deliberate.

David Butler

What I think about the BBC in Northern Ireland – and people here wouldn't disagree with it – BBC Northern Ireland has a peculiar relationship to the society, where it's not responsible, not answerable in a way, because of a peculiar situation. There isn't any political forum in this country – (and BBC Northern Ireland also has the great joy of being removed from the mainland by a pond) – but precisely because there isn't any forum where politicians actually do talk to one another broadcasting has adopted that special role of actually putting the voices on air. It also, because of its brokering role that I am talking about – in the way that it does act as an honest broker – it effectively puts itself above society. The former controller of Northern Ireland (Dick Francis) suggested that impartiality could only be guaranteed by the Britishness of the system ie from outside Northern Ireland, from above the society. That puts BBC Northern Ireland, (less UTV, which has kowtowed), that puts BBC Northern Ireland in a peculiarly vanguardist role. With *The Show*, the mistake, if it was a mistake, was that it got too far ahead of society -it got too far ahead of what was actually riskable. An interesting statistic – there was one vote in the last parliament, the Westminster Parliament on which 16 of 17 Northern Irish MPs voted the same way, Gerry Adams wasn't there, so its hard to say how he would have voted. There was one issue when they all voted the same way and that was David Alton's Abortion Bill. That says much more about the conservatism, ironically about a form of consensus in Northern Ireland than anything I can say about broadcasting.

James Hawthorne

David, if I may respond to your point about the BBC of yesteryear.

Dick Francis *did* say what he said, but he did so fifteen years ago. To Dick I owe, and I think we all owe, an enormous debt of gratitude for his achievements in opening up broadcasting in the BBC in Northern Ireland, but he did make those remarks a long time ago and he also said, as part of the same analysis, that we could never in the BBC in Northern Ireland have a local Broadcasting Council. But views can change and of course, we now have a Broadcasting Council and it has been working extremely well for some years and that may properly answer your proposition about accountability. Now it's easy to assume that the Council has no effect on the actual broadcasting output. I can assure you that it has. Every month the BBC has to meet an independent critical body to discuss its programmes, deliberate, defend and debate issues in the way that we are doing today – though perhaps not as long. And the BBC is accountable through its mail-bag and through its continual interplay with politicians, with both sides of the pond, and with the people of Northern Ireland who definitely address the regional management in a way that very few populations do in the rest of the broadcasting world.

So the BBC *is* accountable and it is ultimately accountable through its own programme output. People can vote with the switch and there are other ways they can react. Witness *The Show* – it's after my time and it may have created problems through its own over-the-top promotion – but it became the hottest newspaper story of the year simply because creative people within the BBC ventured into a new programme format. It's not always an easy passage!

Michael Beattie

Just very briefly, David. You were talking about BBC Northern Ireland just a moment ago, and you made a reference to UTV that I didn't catch.

David Butler

I said that UTV kowtowed. In relation to not screening *Shoot To Kill*.[1] It was an act of craven cowardice.

Michael Beattie

Apart from that example, and I was not directly involved in it so I can't really get into it, I wonder, David, if you perceive any great difference in terms of programme philosophy and practice between BBC Northern Ireland and Ulster Television?

David Butler
Not in terms of news and current affairs, news and current affairs are impeccably good. Not so its treatment of cultural traditions.

Don Anderson
A point of information I just want to say that *Shoot to Kill* was not shown for legal reasons and UTV did not have very much choice in the matter.

David Butler
Well, explain that to me.

Don Anderson
Because Northern Ireland has different jurisdiction, as does Scotland, from England. The programme was showable in England, Scotland and Wales but it was judged to give Ulster Television a problem as publisher in the jurisdiction of Northern Ireland by UTV's legal advisors. I offer that as a piece of information. It is a bit unfair to castigate them for cowardice because they've actually, in some respects, been given very little choice.

Rory Fitzpatrick: Independent Producer
May I come in on David Butler. He made some very interesting academic points but to think these exercise the minds of people who make decisions in broadcasting, or who make the programmes, is totally fallacious.

There are lots of examples that I could give you. Going back 20 years to the Burntollet incident. At that time a paragraph appeared in one of the radical journals saying that a meeting had been held in Ulster Television about the image presented by UTV's coverage of Burntollet. That it had been anti-government etc and it would have to be corrected. It not only told us what was in the meeting, it gave the time of it. I was at that meeting. Nothing of politics was mentioned at all. The only thing that it was concerned with was the loss of equipment to the company by the action that took place, the amount of money that had been lost, the effect of future programming and whether or not it would be wiser to let an organization like ITN take the brunt, rather than have our equipment and our people exposed to it. Now that was what it was about, the story that appeared in the paper had nothing to do with it. There was no discussion about broadcasting philosophy governing the unionists and Ulster Television etc. Can I make another point and this is about the same time. Now there was an awful lot of coverage of Ulster in the early days by both BBC and Independent Television at a national level. This was thought to reflect the very great interest that there was in Ulster. It was thought to be looking at the problems of Ulster, the problem of a divided society, the problem of bigotry, the problem of discrimination. In fact one of the major reasons, and I have heard this expressed by people who knew, who were involved, was that these programmes were infinitely cheaper to make so that in fact if you went to Ulster for one week of your current series you could afford to go to America next week and that was one of the major reasons why so much coverage of Ulster happened in those days.

David Butler

It is not correct to accuse me of saying that UTV or BBC were in league with Stormont or anybody else. In fact I am on record as arguing that the academic analysis which argues that BBC Northern Ireland was in league with Stormont prior to 1968 isn't true.[2] The distinction I am making is between news and current affairs and between treatment of cultural traditions. I think news and current affairs increasingly through the 1960s – and Derek Bailey was right to mention *Flashpoint* as one of the first programmes to introduce analysis to the context – what was there all the way through the 1960s as news was fine. The description was fine, what was missing was analysis.

Martin McLoone

Just a couple of points, suggested by Margo's description of *Hush-a-Bye-Baby* which might lead us on to the final session. I think it is very interesting to consider the response – the quite variable response – to the film within Derry particularly. Now while we often, and quite correctly, emphasise the relationship *between* one community and the other and the need to explain each community to the other and so forth, I think that equally important and valuable and necessary is an exploration *within* each community. An internal exploration, as well as cross-community contact. After all, if there is a freezing of attitudes or an unhealthy fixity about one's sense of identity, then it is within the community, as much as across communities, that one must look for this.

Now I think that it is precisely this that makes *Hush-a-Bye-Baby* such an interesting film. It is an exploration. Now a second point emerges from this, and this is what I was alluding to this morning when I referred to the films I saw at last year's Celtic Film Festival. Where you do have exploration, you are almost, by necessity, *not* going to have bland assertion. You are not going to have the type of film which is going to assert a particular perspective that will immediately be recognisable. Exploration from within unhinges fixed attitudes and therefore is likely to disturb.

If I can use the example of *Hush-a-Bye-Baby* again. For the believing Catholics of Derry's nationalist community, the film doesn't deliver a Catholic text. It explores the relationship of Catholicism, or the contradiction of Catholicism, to the real social realities of young people. The same is true for the republicans in that community – I've heard objections from that quarter and Margo referred to a letter from a person of distinct republican sympathies. Indeed, if you think about militant republican politics and the situation where a person goes out to kill, or to be killed, the last thing they want is exploration – to stop and think about it. What they want is politically assertive backup to what they are doing and, of course, contrary to what some complaints to Channel Four would have it, *Hush-a-Bye-baby* doesn't deliver that either. It is an exploration of the relationship between that republican tradition and other influences, especially in regard to women. In other words the various contradictory forces that operate within it.

So two points then. One, that exploration within the community seems to me to be an important factor and two, that one of the inevitable, but necessary, by-products of this is that a lot of people will reject this because it does not assert the way they might see that community.

Margo Harkin

Just to correct you, Martin, on one point. In fact the issues that are discussed in *Hush-a-bye-Baby* are very much issues that are discussed in the republican movement, in feminist and socialist groupings in Ireland. The issues of women's rights were issues that we discussed and I think the kind of responses that were negative to that came from within the right wing. I mean I don't even like using these terms but you know those kind of elements in that particular society or grouping and in the broader nationalist grouping which doesn't involve itself day to day with ordinary people. People are not aware of what those debates are because they don't hear them so I just want to correct that. In a sense that film was actually representing a debate which is not normally heard or is assumed not to take place within those particular groupings and the people who defended the film came from those same groupings.

Now I just have another wee quote that I want to give you here. When it went out on Channel Four, a woman from Belfast rang up and said the language was disgusting, the programme didn't present a fair view of the children of Northern Ireland, it ran down the British army and didn't do justice to what *normal* children think of the army. That is kind of mind-blowing to me – that there is somebody who thinks that people who don't like the British army are not normal. That the behaviour is aberrant in some way. I am not advocating that, women like that, people like her, ought to be strapped to a chair and made to watch these programmes. Obviously not, but I am very happy that she saw it because there is a sense of racism about her letter. That there is something unseemly about this culture which she was exposed to on TV. I think the more people actually see other people's culture and recognise it and don't be so hypocritical about the fact that it actually isn't reflecting something in their own experience as well, then the better.

Des Cranston

Thank you Margo. Now would any member of the panel like to make a concluding comment or should we just finish there? On your behalf then, let me thank the panel for a series of contrasting and stimulating talks which certainly elicited some interesting responses. Thank you all.

Notes

1 *Shoot to Kill,* dir: Peter Kosminsky, Yorkshire Television. This is a dramatic account of the circumstances surrounding the inquiry into an alleged 'shoot to kill' policy set up under the chairmanship of John Stalker and the circumstances surrounding Stalker's later removal from the inquiry. The programme was transmitted on June 3rd and 4th 1990, but not shown in Northern Ireland. The programme has not yet been screened by RTE and a proposed screening in August 1991 was cancelled. It therefore remains unseen in Ireland, north and south.

2 The analysis referred to here is in Liz Curtis, *Ireland : The Propaganda War,* London, Pluto Press, 1984. It is refuted in David Butler, 'Ulster Unionism and British Broadcasting Journalism 1924-89' in Bill Rolston (ed), *The Media and Northern Ireland : Covering the Troubles,* London, Macmillan, 1991.

SESSION 4

Chair: John Hill

Media Studies, UUC

OPEN FORUM: WHAT IS TO BE DONE?

Right, if I can have your attention please. It's my job to chair the final session. When we were drawing lots for the chairman's roles for today I drew the short straw. While everybody else was able to come on and give a fulsome welcome to the many guests on the platform, I was, as you can see from the programme, allocated a chairman's role without having anyone to introduce. However, by way of a compromise I've enlisted two people, not to welcome but to give a second welcome to. On my right we've got James Hawthorne and on my left Martin McLoone. Now there is some point in bringing them back to the platform other than to give me the opportunity to have someone to welcome. This is because the event, as you'll know, is sponsored by the Cultural Traditions Group in association with Media Studies. In his opening remarks, Martin described the experience of being a member of the Cultural Traditions Media Group, a body which has money to spend, modest amounts admittedly, but money nonetheless. And, in a sense, today's event was provoked by that media group's deliberations about what sort of programmes this money should be given to. Given that the group's remit is to support programmes that are, in some way, addressing or in dialogue with local cultural traditions, it seemed quite important to have a symposium where we interrogated both the notion of culture and the notion of tradition. I've invited Martin and Jimmy back, therefore, not only to see if they have learned anything during the course of the day, and whether they are better people as a result of our deliberations, but also to give you the opportunity to share your thoughts with them and perhaps for them to respond to the comments that may be made from the floor.

Now it is designated an open discussion because there is a diverse group of people here today from different sections of broadcasting and film and video production and we want to try and open up the debate to include as many people as possible rather than privilege the people on the platform. However in my role as chairman perhaps I could beg your indulgence just for a few minutes to try and raise one or two questions that we might address ourselves to. You will notice that our open discussion is entitled 'Film making and Broadcasting – what is to be done?' I felt rather pleased that I had smuggled in the 'what is to be done' phrase which many of you will recognise as the title of a classic work by Lenin. However James Hawthorne was so quick to spot this that I wonder if there is some substance after all to Tory allegations of marxist entryism into the BBC. This issue aside, however, I now want to focus the discussion on this and related questions: of what sort of broadcasting, and what sort of film and video production we have had experience of, whether we approve or disapprove of it, and what sort of work we should now like to see and encourage.

In the last session, there was a certain tension emerging between the broadcasters and the academics. To use Derek Bailey's words, programme makers have to 'press on' making the things and its only academics in our ivory tower who can afford the indulgence of critical reflection. However, it seems to me that it is important that programme makers do engage in a dialogue with academics, that they do not simply press on making things all the time but also take time out now and again to reflect on whether they could be making things differently, whether they could be making things in a better way, and whether they should take on board the sort of questions that people have been raising today. It was Michael Beattie, of UTV, who gave us a description of what he would like to see, and I think of what we would all probably like to see, and that was 'deeper, more radical programmes'. I wonder whether we could now address just what this might mean, what deeper and more radical programmes might consist of and how the cultural traditions media group might best encourage them. To make two comments about this.

Although Michael introduced this phrase, he almost immediately became defensive and said yes we would like to make these deeper, more radical programmes but its a question of money and therefore not always possible. The question of *quality* and of course the issue of the impending ITC quality threshold then came to the fore. Now it seems to me that we should be vary wary of the way in which we use the concept of quality because quality, as Michael rightly pointed out in the context of the ITC licences, is often only a substitute term for variety and a range of scheduling. Similarly it seems to me that broadcasters have also traditionally used the notion of quality as being in some way synonymous with money and have worked on the assumption that if you throw money at a film or programme it will necessarily be better. However, one of the lessons provided by the independents that have been transmitted by Channel Four is that quality is not necessarily synonymous with the amount of money you spend on a production. You can make a lot of rubbish with a lot of money but you can also make very good programmes on very modest budgets and, therefore, if we are to talk sensibly about quality it is important that we separate it from the issue of finance. The idea of quality should really be much more to do with the content, the form and mode of address of a work, to do with the way that it takes on board particular issues and the way that it deals with them. Money cannot substitute, in this respect, for good ideas, intelligence and imagination.

The second point is the one that has been recurring throughout the day. In Northern Ireland where outside media images of the province have been so extensive and powerful the importance of local indigenous work is self-evident. But how should local producers approach and deal with local cultural traditions? Two sorts of answers appear to have emerged during the day.

The first might be labelled the equal opportunities approach which has stressed the diversity of cultural traditions and the need for these to be fairly and equally represented in the media. One of the weaknesses of this approach, it has been argued, however, is that it simply accepts cultural traditions as discrete and fixed identities and, in doing so, encourages what David Butler has described as a 'stand off' situation in which different cultural traditions may enjoy equal representation but do not enter into any dialogue either with themselves or each other.

This leads to the second approach which has argued for the importance of work which attempts to move beyond the kind of pregiven, already existing differences and divisions characteristic of Northern Ireland but in a way which neither attempts to ignore or sanitise the very real divisions that do exist or to project some imaginary, or madly utopian, resolution of them. The challenge here is to make programmes, films and videos which do not simply reflect pre-given cultural identities and traditions but which also seek to explore and investigate these same cultural traditions. It was this idea of the internal exploration of cultural traditions with which Martin began the day and it seems to me to be an important one to hold on to even though it does mean, as Mickey McGowan appeared to lament, that film makers and broadcasters are unable then simply to represent their community. I'm not convinced, however, that there ever is an unproblematic set of cultural attitudes or community interests to represent or that even community film and video groups can expect to be straightforward representatives of them. Indeed, it seems to me to be important that while work should emerge out of and seek to do justice to different communities and cultural traditions it should not expect, or wish, to do so in an unquestioning manner.

Finally it has been noticeable that we have not actually looked at any film and video material. When we organised this event we did think about the possibility of showing material as there is something slightly rarefied about having a one day symposium on broadcasting and film and television and not actually having any examples in front of us. However one of the problems that we then had was deciding what to show. Any selection of material would inevitably privilege some programmes at the expense of others and possibly lead to complaints of various types. Our solution, then, was not to show anything at all. Despite this, however, it still seems appropriate that we should talk about programmes that we both like and dislike as one means of making our deliberations on what is to be done more concrete.

I'm conscious that I've spoken rather longer than I intended. Could I now, therefore, invite people to make contributions from the floor and, perhaps, engage with some the issues I've suggested.

Jimmy Brown: Making Media Work

In addressing what is to be done and, as we have seen in the last workshop in terms of broadcasting and film making in a divided community, I think we need to look at how the community is divided, why and by whom and if we ignore those facts then we are setting ourselves some problems. One of the earlier speakers addressed the fact of broadcasters needing to satisfy their audience and I think if we set that against Bob Collins and his notion of the pervasive sense of commercial values I think you see very clearly the case of he who pays the piper calls the tune (or makes the video or film, whatever the case may be). It is here that I agree with David Butler when he says there is no neutral language, verbal or visual, and it is the case that in any epoch it is the ruling ideas which prevail. By banning or censoring political opponents or by portraying them as something other than normal or ordinary as Bob Collins says in RTE that they attempted to do in their coverage of the North in recent years, I think you are in danger of ignoring the real polemic and dialectic that comes out of the contradictions that David Butler spoke of. As far as my contribution to Making Media Work we are about trying to empower people in the community. People want the skills of media and want to use them within the community. What we are also asking of the Cultural Traditions Group is that, in considering what they should do and what is to be done, they should now lobby actively for an end to censorship. Words never killed anybody, whatever group. Peoples attitudes to violence differ and we should be free in what we have to say.

John Hill

I wonder, Jimmy, would you have a comment on that, given that the Cultural Traditions Group do, I think, have a criterion that they would normally expect work that is submitted to be broadcastable or likely to be broadcast and thus may be seen, at least implicity, to be condoning censorship.

James Hawthorne

Perhaps in this assembly, the Cultural Traditions Group is known for the help or the subsidy we have given to projects which have subsequently gone out on BBC or Ulster Television. But we are also interested, and have stated our interest in, the use of video, in whatever form, within communities and especially if it can be seen by other communities. There is most certainly much creative and artistic potential in communities and traditionally we might think of that creativity expressing itself through community theatre. But why not through video where technical costs are now much reduced? So when we hear of a likely project we feel we should assist the process of community and cross-community expression. In other words, at one end we are interested in assisting a particular kind of professional television and film which will address large audiences but at the other end we are interested in the use of video at grass roots level. And if anyone here knows of a project that might look at the problems we are interested in, sitting within six feet of you is Dr Maurna Crozier and Maurna will supply you with the required form to state your case, why you require a subsidy, what is your overall purpose and the chances are you'll find us very sympathetic to any effective community or inter-community proposal. The help is there.

Jimmy Brown

If I can just respond here. The point I am making is why can't you give people in the community the skills and how to use them? We have a situation if someone who may have a particular political orientation and has something to say within a community , he has to be excluded if the thing is to be broadcast anywhere. What I am saying is I think a group such as yourselves could be more vocal, verbal or visual in perhaps opposing the whole notion of censorship in television.

James Hawthorne

Well that raises a question about how the Community Relations Council does its work and what style it adopts. We took an early decision that we didn't want to be seen as yet another passionate peace-loving group – I hope I'm not being unkind to any particular group -tempted to issue statements after every atrocity. We see disadvantages in entering the debate in a high-profile, foreshortened manner. I believe we can exert our influence in other more effective ways. On the question of censorship, and in the particular recent incident involving Glor na nGael[1], we should not underestimate the role that the Council has played in helping to solve the more general problem in the short and longer term. Such action is unlikely to be reported in the Andytown News, the Irish News or the Belfast Telegraph, but it certainly is possible to contribute effectively to a public debate without resorting to clarion calls. There is scope for our particular style and we are prepared to work hard and insist on results.

Paul Nolan: Workers Educational Association

I think it is accepted the CRC does a lot of its work behind the scenes, but I think it would be useful also if in this area of subsidising media production, if you could be more explicit in what your criteria actually are. In other words what is it you are trying to do? Is it to foster community relations in the sense I think you just put it – to help one community understand the other or could it be the internal exploration that Martin McLoone was speaking about earlier or is it both and if so is there any order of priority there for you?

A second question is do you have any way of evaluating your work, of knowing if any of these things actually achieve the ends that you hope they will? Do they in any sense better community relations? Do you know?

James Hawthorne

I'll take your point about community development versus inter-community activity, or is it a mixture of both? I think the short answer is that we are likely to be interested in both but, as always, there's a bit of background. Community Development has been temporarily out of fashion, in political terms, and we took note of that when we were forming our Community Relations Council. As it happened, we were very busy initially with a new inter-community agenda. But what we have been saying, and I have said it to the Minister and I continue to say it in other places, is that you can't always achieve inter-community interest without first having some sense of one's own community. Where that does not exist, then it will have to be fostered so that it may progress to something else. So we look sympathetically at projects which, initially, may have no inter-community dimension but where we judged it might develop later. So to some extent, and to answer part of your question, we are interested in both kinds of community development.

You raised the point of evaluation. We shall have to develop evaluation techniques in the future, but quite honestly, in our first year, we have had to exercise judgement and common sense and hope and, in some cases, set a few doubts aside. We've been happy on occasions to give the benefit of the doubt. We do know – it can only be a gut feeling – that those who have been attempting interesting and new things and perhaps trying to express themselves through film and video, and through publishing, are feeling a little happier and more encouraged now that there is a new body taking an interest in their work and perhaps that's an indication of progress. Doubtless, accountants will soon appear and take the square root of everything in sight and they'll be talking about, you know, 'value for money'. It's going to be difficult to evaluate success in those terms and my feeling, Paul, is that we shouldn't rush it. That might be a touch unscientific but I believe that enough of us have been around for a long time to know that there's a backlog of ideas and great scope for experiment. Let's address those and maybe, three years from now, we can have a monster debate here in Coleraine to start a proper evaluation. In fact we should be grateful if someone would start working on a methodology.

Don Anderson: ITC

When you ask, John, what is to be done, everything depends on resources, everything depends on money. I am wondering what actually happens here, maybe we are a very shy lot. I see the Welsh have got S4C. I see in Scotland, the Gallic language has been given 9.5 million for injection for Gallic programming. Now that's a cultural tradition, we haven't got anything like that in Northern Ireland. I don't know what your budget is Jimmy, but it might be in the order of £100,000. Do you think that there also should be pressure for that kind of money on a pro rata basis that might be something like 2.5 million pounds for programme makers here. Do you think there ought to be pressure for that and would it be something you would like to administer?

James Hawthorne

Beware of the 'pro rata' argument. Answers that look attractive arithmetically may be a bit embarrassing. But I would acknowledge your point. Look at the case of S4C in Wales which actually received financial assistance from Scottish and Ulster Television. How the Welsh got away with that arrangement is a story in itself. But remember that the Welsh are part of the swing of British politics. We are not. But I take your general point that there is actually no reason why Northern Ireland cannot deploy, at least to some degree, the pro rata argument. But how should the money be spent? In television terms, what would be a realistic request that the public at large would accept? I am not going to defend the policy of the BBC throughout its history on this issue, except to say that in my own time we did not take a few quantum leaps. And now through the Council we will continue to promote imaginative ideas and we have done so.

I should add, with regard to grants and resources generally, that in the first year, not all our available money was taken up under some headings. I have said we were prepared to give the benefit of the doubt but we nevertheless evaluate ideas very carefully. We haven't yet got our machinery into gear but I would dare to say that there is actually no shortage of money for decent projects. Now that Tony McCusker has left this hall, and noting that he is a civil servant, the Central Community Relations Unit have been extraordinarily sympathetic. Where we overran in some areas we got additional funding. The argument that there hasn't been enough money to do what needed to be done has simply got to be re-examined.

John Patterson

Two points, in connection with the question of what is to be done. Firstly considering the fact, as John Hill pointed out, big budgets don't necessarily mean good programmes. Perhaps the role of public service broadcasters, and I include UTV in this, perhaps their role should change. Instead of trying to compete on an entertainment basis with the new satellite channels perhaps they should move towards commissioning systems like Channel Four, but on a much smaller scale, geared towards the immediate area. If you are an independent commercial company in a specific region, perhaps you should fund small scale production within that region that would deal with issues that are of concern to that region. That would be one way of moving forward. Also independents who are making programmes, should make them with some kind of real investigation and interrogation of what those communities are, giving access to the kinds of voices which are seldom heard.

Michael Beattie

A very brief point in response to Jimmy. Actually the thought crossed my mind whenever Margo was speaking earlier. Whenever

Margo was sitting frustrated in Derry before Channel Four came along, had she ever approached Ulster Television? Now it may well be the case that she may have done that, maybe others have done that and I am not aware of it, but sometimes I get sick to the back teeth with complaints about Ulster Television from people who have never come near us to suggest projects or show us the kind of material that they are working on. It's not purely on any kind of concerns about the broadcasting restrictions or whatever that we make programme judgements. Someone may come to us with a programme which is so poor technically or lacking in creative quality that we don't want to have it about us but at least if they came to us they would know our reaction to that. I would have to say that there are students (I don't know if they are currently in the room but they were earlier on) who have benefitted in terms of cash and resources from UTV because they came to us. I have to tell you that the first meeting I had with Belfast Film Workshop was at my instigation, the first official meeting I had with Belfast Independent Video (or Northern Visions as they are now) was at my instigation and I think that too often people are inclined to criticise broadcasters from outside without ever having actually approached the broadcasters.

John Hill

I think it would be fair to say that partly you have been inspired by Channel Four's example and its only recently, with the stipulation of the 25% quota coming from independents, that UTV is adopting more open door policies.

Michael Beattie

To a degree yes.

Margo Harkin

Yes I think it is now, but I want to say, for the record, that *Hush-a-Bye-Baby* was submitted to UTV and was turned down.

Johnny Gogan: Film Base, Dublin

Film Base in Dublin is a facility which was set up by film makers to serve their own needs; their training and equipment and infor-

mation needs. I would actually like to go back to the start, where
Philip Schlesinger started, talking about the global issues as well as
the community discussion after lunch. I think what is going on in
Ireland at present, and I think that we need to look at what is
actually happening on a 32 county basis, I think the point of the
discussion has very much been centred on the six counties, we
need to analyse what is actually happening nationally in the context of the global situation. There is a kind of cultural paralysis
which grips the whole country in a sense. We are living with this
great change taking place with a sense of powerlessness at how to
confront this change. We're living in a very closeted way. Film
makers in the south tend to be a very, very marginal group within
the arts. We have been overwhelmed, really, by production that
comes into the country from Hollywood-based production companies. There are perhaps 21 films geared to be shot in Ireland, in
the south, in the next year. Most of these might not necessarily
come but there is no indigenous production of the type of film,
like *Hush-a-Bye Baby* set to happen because that area of production
has been totally neglected, both on the part of government and
broadcasters – by RTE, partly because it hasn't got any money,
partly because it doesn't really have a dynamic policy and also by
the Dublin Government who have axed the Irish Film Board,
really out of financial reasons but also from a type of anti-intellectual attitude because they didn't like the productions coming out
of it. I think this is a similar thing to what is happening in the north
– a suspicion of people who are trying to find the way forward, are
trying to see into the future – the way in fact that Margo's film
actually was a real Irish film but actually expressed a lot to people
throughout Ireland which a lot of the TV programmes just don't
do. I think there needs to be a lot more cooperation between film
makers in the north and film makers in the south, both in terms of
developing funding structures within Ireland but also in dealing
with this MEDIA 1992 initiative, a project of the European Commission which is providing over the next five years, I think, 200
million pounds for film development, for audio visual development.[2] This funding, for the film makers in the South, is more
important than funding that actually emanates from within Ireland and I think that unless we actually develop a funding structure within Ireland to make our own films we are going to be
overwhelmed by American culture, by British culture. Irish film
makers have increasingly had problems raising money in Britain

because of the political situation, because of the financial crisis in British film making and I think that has to be addressed. I would like the discussion to move to look at Ireland a bit more as one entity and I realise that is something the politicians just aren't doing but the film makers are going to have to do so.

Helen Doherty: Media Worker, Birmingham

I want to try and draw together a couple of connections and then suggest something that I think should be done. I would also like to say that this is informed by my past work as an arts administrator with a regional arts association, dispensing film funding, and also as a media educationalist. But first of all, I saw *Mother Ireland* in Birmingham shortly after it was banned in a small cinema and the group of people who watched it didn't speak for something like 30 seconds or so afterwards because it had such impact on them. I think with the Irish in Birmingham it was actually even more important, and I am not suggesting that films ought to be banned, what I am saying it got seen in that context and it maybe had more impact in that situation than it might have had being simply part of a film programme. But subsequently I saw *Hush-a-Bye Baby* on television for the second time and that was quite important in British cultural terms. It seems to me important to discuss not just the things that can be done but also the things that had been done and if there are role models around, the organizations and the women who were involved in making those two films are just that. Thank you to them and the assistance of Channel Four. But language is a key point in what many of us talk about and one word, especially, that John Hill referred to – *quality*. I think there has been another definition of quality – a subtext used by broadcasters in the context of professionalism. Professionalism has quite often been used as a block to people as far as the BBC, and independent television companies, are concerned, indeed quite often Channel Four as well which has developed its own language, its own style, so I think we should actually recognise that notions of quality, actually set up blocks between the institutions and those film makers of quality who have good ideas. Are they *your* good ideas? Is it those ideas which *you* recognise as quality which dictate what is made or shown? So the first thing I would suggest is some sort of public forum on language. Just to introduce ideas about how to approach the funding bodies, how much paper, how does it need to be presented, what are the varying levels of script or outlines which are needed to actually get people through the doors, or elicit some sort of favourable reception? So that is actually quite a practical point which I don't think will be expensive and I am sure quite a few of the people here, and from radio as well, would be quite willing to do that. It might result in much greater numbers of ideas, of better quality, eventually coming through.

I would also suggest that you recognise, given that there is no dedicated Irish film school for productions, that quite a lot of the film projects that you get are training-on-the-job and in a way the production funding that you may give is also training funding and I think that's quite an important point. The third and final thing that I would like to say is that I don't think that you can legislate for innovation, you can just hope that you get risk-taking innovative projects through and perhaps you should privilege those which are risk-taking in cultural terms over those which can get funded elsewhere.

Simon Woods

Yes I just want to make some comments about the fact that the Cultural Traditions Group has a budget for film, videos and tv programmes. For a long time it has been clear that the level of funding available in the north for independent film makers is appalling – the BFI doesn't operate here, the Arts Council said that the reason they don't fund film and production is because it covers too many arts subjects already. The local authorities here, with the wonderful exception Derry and to a small extent Belfast, have never funded film or video so we are in an iniquitous position, especially when compared to Wales, Scotland or England.

Without trying to denigrate what Jimmy's doing, it seems a bit like Cultural Traditions has become flavour of the month and all of a sudden there's money there for film, TV programmes that fit in with that sort of remit. But I don't think that really helps create a film, video, or television culture particularly because it may have died on its feet before you arrive. It just seems that if there is no encouragement in general for people to get involved in making films and videos or whatever, in general outside of it being for a specific section of the cultural divisions, then I am not surprised you haven't spent the money this year because people aren't going to just pop up and say, 'Oh great! Now lets get down to it.' They've gone on and done something else, they've gone somewhere else to do it – the traditional Irish method of finding employment. It just seems to be side-stepping the issue to a certain extent. Are you worried for instance that it gives the government an out for saying they don't have to create some equivalent of the BFI?

Catherine O'Neill

In the last two years I have worked at the Edinburgh International Television Festival – now its not a festival its a closed conference, a delegate only conference – and the level of debate at it is very, very poor. It's almost banal -with two exceptions. Two conferences ago I attended, as a steward, *A Question of Censorship* in 1989. At it we had Peter Robinson, Conor Cruise O'Brien, Eamon McCann and it was very good, being chaired by Barry Cowan. Now the fact that we had those people sitting down at a table talking to each other was brilliant and it was not just me, in my little naive Northern Irish way who thought it was a good debate. It was in fact seen as the best to be held at the festival. Again in 1990 the best debate, I thought, was the debate on the drama – documentary where we had Peter Kosminsky who I think was director of *Shoot to Kill*,[3] we had someone from Panorama, we had Roger Bolton from Thames Television and we had Tom McGurk who wrote *Dear Sarah*[4] and it again was the best. You wouldn't believe how terrible the other debates were. I mean people were falling asleep and leaving in their droves at this supposed international television festival but was it coincidence that these two debates which were the best in both years just happened to be about Northern Ireland. I don't think it was coincidence, I think there is something about broadcasting in Northern Ireland, the tensions that exist here, that make for good broadcasting. Also at the TV festival, basically if you are intellectual and you want to get in you have got a pretty hard job! Its really for broadcasters and if you are from a university you cannot get in. What I can say is this conference today is absolutely important. There should be more of them. I don't know how isolated this is but I certainly wouldn't have heard of it if Philip Schlesinger hadn't invited me to come along. I think there should be more debates like this with broadcasters and people from their ivory towers who get together because we can learn so much from each other and that's all I would like to say.

John Hill
Jimmy, I would like you to respond to these points.

James Hawthorne
I feel like a shepherd on a steep hill whose the sheep have all broken loose. How do I get them back?

If I sound defensive – he said, beating his breast – I don't mean to be. I will try to clarify some points.

Many points strike home and I welcome them as fresh ideas. If I may start critically... John Patterson: I think if we were to accept your formula for how the money of the institutional broadcasters should be spent, we should have been brought to our financial knees in the BBC in a very short time, trying to execute that marvellous philosophy of yours. One of the difficulties that will forever face the BBC, which has to be seen as the 'national instrument of broadcasting' is that in order to defend its right to a licence fee from every family in the country, it has to provide a broadly popular service with a good supply of light entertainment. If it becomes, as some people are wont to recommend, a more exclusive specialised organisation, then its demand for a nationally based licence is seriously – and quite properly – questioned. And that's the dilemma and I'll leave it at that if I may.

I was fascinated, Margo, as we all were, by your thrilling account of the difficulties you experienced in trying to make films. If I might make one observation; whilst you can delineate the short-comings of the Establishment, the most crucial failure was in the 'Irish' area. Institutional broadcasters have to address vast audiences and deep layers of prejudice. Martin reminds us of the theme 'What should be done?' but let us remind ourselves that most consumers of broadcasting are *Sun* readers! When I returned to this country from Hong Kong in 1978, I discovered that the BBC's most popular programme in Northern Ireland, and *only* in Northern Ireland, was *The Dukes of Hazzard*, indicating our cultural leanings towards go-faster stripes and Country and Western music. It was a runaway winner. So, when you are creating fine programmes to stimulate a large audience intellectually, do bear in mind what they really want if only to survive professionally. Yet, ultimately, you do want to address that audience and achieve an impact.

Johnny's point about cultural paralysis: quite honestly Johnny I cannot fully share your view. We are coming out of our cultural coma in the North and many of us are seeing signs of movement. There's a burgeoning interest, for example, in local history and that is not finding expression on the screen. We've a new school curriculum – I know it started in the Conservative Central Office – but it travelled strangely well across the Irish Sea. Fortuitously, it was worked on and translated into local priorities by decent people in local Education. I, for one, warmly commend the result.

We have Rotha and Carol from LEDU – the Local Enterprise Development Unit which has links with IDB, the Industrial Development Board. Both Rotha and Carol were here today and I have to say that they've been to every conference recently held on ways of improving and supporting film, hoping for workable, supportable ideas from the film-makers and ready to help. If I am told that there are communication problems over the funding of film, I think those who make films have to assume a greater share of the blame than those with the declared willingness to help. What the well-wishers require are clear messages about what kind of help that is specifically required.

As to the question of our being overwhelmed by American and British culture, that is not a sole North-Irish problem. We all had hopes once of how television would educate and change the world. What we actually got was *The Streets of San Francisco* dubbed into Swahili. We suffer less than most countries because of the strength of our indigenous programme making.

However, Helen-Doherty-from-Birmingham – I'm beginning to sound like a DJ – if I can give you a reply to some of your points; you make a very crucial point when you identify the need actually to teach people how to apply to, and therefore get the best use of, organisations such as the Cultural Traditions Group. The evidence is that many individuals and groups have good ideas locked away and simply lack the gumption to master the process of application. Very often, if and when they apply, they make out a very weak case and we actually spend a lot of time with them encouraging some degree of self-belief.

You also raised the point about training. We have in fact thought of that and in other branches of our Community Relations work we have made a reasonable start. Indeed every course we have run so far has been over-subscribed. LEDU and IDB are also interested in training needs. It's essential that we identify what training is required.

A point has been made about innovation. I will perhaps join with John over here. We don't want to narrow the scope. We don't want to dictate. We are not saying that if you broadcast certain wholesome ideas you will get money and if you don't you won't! But we are not a general Film Board and we *are* selective in that we have recognised that film – media generally – is part of our culture and we believe it should contribute to the crucial needs which many of us have been trying to identify. But we are open to do business with individual film makers who have their own views and to join those whose ideas are innovative, liberal and creative. There are specific ideas in which we are interested and we shall be open about those but we don't want to prescribe and if you find us guilty you will no doubt let us know.

The BFI has been raised! Some wretched lawyer, when the organisation was being founded years ago, got his constitutional grammar wrong and the British Film Institute – pledged to serve the nation – had no remit in Northern Ireland. That tiresome problem is being addressed and about every three weeks I am in London within the very portals of the BFI and perhaps, if the UK Screen Commission comes into being, we shall at last get a place in the sun.[5]

The debates in Edinburgh have been well described. There is much strutting by the senior executives of the industry at these debates but I suspect there's a slight shortage of agenda. I did a piece in Edinburgh a few years ago and there wasn't a dry eye but that was because Northern Ireland was the only worthwhile topic in the entire conference, it being a kind of microcosm of the whole dilemma of balance in broadcasting.

I take a lot of important points away from this conference and I thank you for them. Getting more films actually made here will require further study and we will promise to help in the closing of gaps to ensure that more can be achieved. We do need television and films that can contribute to a wider understanding of ourselves and it will be a privilege to assist in the creative and innovative process.

I needn't protest how strongly I feel about the so-called 'ban'. It strikes me as more than slightly bizarre that we can watch and listen to Saddam Hussein and his apologists, strutting around our screens, revolver-armed and creating false images and sickening propaganda, and yet we seem to require protection from certain, albeit fairly duplicitous, elected representatives.

I hope I have not been defensive. I have found our discussion valuable.

John Hill

Just one point regarding the need for a clearer Northern Ireland film policy. There is, of course, the Northern Ireland Film Council which represents a significant body of film and television workers and has been developing a coherent and integrated policy for film and television production, training, distribution, exhibition, education and archive in Northern Ireland.[6] The messages regarding what is to be done about films and video are not, perhaps, as confused as you're suggesting. However, I think it is about time we should wrap up and I would just like to take the opportunity to thank our two panellists and offer Martin the opportunity to sum up his responses.

Martin McLoone

Well, I remained quiet while Jimmy was rounding up all his straying sheep so maybe now is the time for me to have a little bleat.

In laying out the structure for today's event, I made a bet with myself that we could go through the day without getting caught up in questions of funding – or the economics of film-making in general. Well, I lost that bet. Despite the fact that one of the framing ideas for the symposium was the fact that the Cultural Traditions Group does have money and that we wish to consult the film makers, broadcasters and independents about how best this money might be spent, we very quickly went back into discussing the general lack of infrastructure in regard to an audio-visual industry in Ireland.

Well, that perhaps, was to be expected. I am aware of the problems here and have written forcibly in the past about the lack of just such an infrastructure[7] and maybe until some kind of basic funding and production framework is in place, perhaps my ambition that we discuss the kinds of films, videos or TV programmes we should *aspire* to make, will have to wait.

But remember, that Cultural Traditions funding is in place and must be spent. The remit – that projects must somehow explore cultural traditions (I prefer the phraseology questions of identity) – is a broad criterion.

Nothing is either included or excluded. I've indicated the types
of programmes which I would like to emerge. Internal explora-
tions of identity, emanating from within communities themselves.
I agree with David Butler, that perhaps we have had too much
bland folklore – nostalgic escapes into idealised pasts, which seem
to be so much a part of cultural production, not just here, but as I
indicated this morning, throughout the so-called Celtic periphery.
These kinds of programmes have their uses, but they will be made
anyway, so perhaps we should look to balance these with slightly
more contemporary, risk-taking programming. There seemed to
be a fair amount of support throughout the day for that kind of
approach, I was happy to note.

Simon Woods is right when he says that there is little or no
infrastructure for production here. But, you know, an audio-visual
culture is about more than just funding and production arrangements. We in Northern Ireland especially, have a very media-
conscious society – we have, all of us, well-developed antennae for
picking up nuances – but I don't think that amounts to a *media-
literate* society. Part of the culture we are referring to – part of the
infrastructure – must also be an educational one. And part of that
process is interrogating what has been done and looking for ways
of improving, developing or moving beyond these. As John has
indicated, this is not always a matter of finance or funding – very
few of the expensive, costume dramas which were so much a part
of TV fiction over the last ten years, actually amounted to very
much, in my opinion – I would argue the case for RTE's *Strumpet
City* and one or two others – but relatively inexpensive TV fictions,
like BBC Northern Ireland's *Elephant*[8] for example, much criti-
cised but also much praised, can extract a far greater response
from audiences because they try to be different, try to explore in
different ways.

So I come back to my main theme of the day. Yes, we do need
adequate funding and training. Yes, TV production and film making is expensive, but we cannot go on for ever talking *only* about
these matters and not discuss in detail what that funding and
training will actually produce – programmes, videos and films.

We rarely discuss or analyse these in our schools, we rarely
provide the kind of exhibition which allows this to happen in
public – we rarely get together the producers, aspiring producers,
consumers, critics or academics who might push a more reflective
approach. And this in a society ripped apart by communal strife

and division and which is perhaps the most photographed, video-taped, filmed and audio-recorded in the Western World! It seems crazy to me.

I enjoyed today's discussions, nonetheless, and was pleased that the speakers who agreed to stimulate discussion, took their task seriously and provided food for thought. On your behalf, I would like to thank them all. Even if my final question – What is to be done? – remains in the air, nonetheless, a lot of opinion, information and underlying philosophy did emerge and I would express my thanks to everyone who turned up today and joined in this process. In the end, over one hundred and twenty people visited us today for this symposium, not counting the University staff and students who dropped by. This is an astounding number, I think, and demonstrates that these issues tax a lot of people's minds. We should perhaps aim to so something similar again, perhaps next time screening some material and trying to draw out some of the issues this raises.

I think as well, that the European dimension to our own local difficulties, over identity and over broadcasting, will continue to be relevant throughout this decade, so I have no doubt that we will be discussing these again.

John Hill

On that note, I think its appropriate to stop. Despite Martin's reservations, it has been a successful day and I am confident that the issues raised will continue to be discussed and debated.

I would like to thank Martin McLoone for organising the event, Media Studies at the University of Ulster for hosting it and the Cultural Traditions Group for funding it. I'd also like to thank all of you for attending and for making today's event so lively.

There's been a lot of discussion today about cultural traditions and the need not only to give them expression but also to subject them to critical scrutiny. However, I'd now like to invite you to participate – relatively uncritically – in a longstanding cultural tradition and join us for a drink. Wine will be served in the Terrace Dining Room and everyone is welcome. Thank you.

NOTES

1   Glor na nGael is a community based group in Belfast, set up to promote the Irish language. In 1990, Government funding was withdrawn, according to

the Secretary of State for Northern Ireland because of alleged para-military connections. Glor na nGael have appealed the decision.

2 For a discussion of the various MEDIA initiatives, see Part 1 above.

3 *Shoot to Kill,* dir: Peter Kosminsky, Yorkshire Television, first transmitted June 3rd and 4th 1990, but not shown in Northern Ireland.

4 *Dear Sarah,* dir: Frank Cvitanovich, wr: Tom McGurk, RTE, 1990. Based on the letters of Guiseppe Conlon, one of the Maguire Seven, convicted of complicity in the Birmingham bombings of 1974, who died in prison in 1980. Subsequently the convictions were quashed.

5 In March 1991, the Board of Governors passed a motion amending the BFI's Charter to include Northern Ireland and this amendment received Royal approval in May 1991. It remains to be seen what this will mean for film culture in Northern Ireland in the long term. One short term result is that the BFI's annual Easter School, for teachers of media studies, is scheduled to take place in Northern Ireland for the first time, in April 1992.

6 In June 1991, the NIFC published *Strategy Proposals for the Development of the Film, Television and Video Industries and Culture in Northern Ireland.* This was widely distributed to relevant industrial and cultural bodies and negotiations about future developments are proceeding.

7 Martin McLoone, 'ACNI-culture : A Blurred Vision', *CIRCA,* No.39, Mar/ Apr.1988.

8 *Elephant,* dir: Alan Clarke, BBC NI, transmitted 25 January 1989.

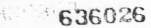